WORKBOOK PRESS LLC
187 E Warm Springs Rd,
Suite B285 Las Vegas NV 89119 USA

Website: https://workbookpress.com/
Hotline: 1-888-818-4856
Email: admin@workbookpress.com

Ordering Information:

Quantity sales. Special discounts are available on quantity purchases by corporations, associations, and others. For details, contact the publisher at the address above.

Library of Congress Control Number:

ISBN-13:   978-1-965732-31-1   Paperback Version

REV. DATE: 12/24/2024

WHY DID I Start Trucking?

Khafra Akbar

INTRODUCTION

HERE'S A WONDERFUL STORY OF when I Mr. K came to a point in my life when I wanted to change the way I Was living and change my financial income in my life. So I could be more supportive in my life for my self and my family. So my family didn't have to struggle. So I searched for a number of different things to try and do and experience a different way of life and in business. To were I didn't have to gamble when it was time to pay any bills. Not making a consistent amount of income a month can be stressful so I set out to find a occupation that I would find interest in. Also can provide an income that I was looking for which was to support me and my family. As I searched for this new way of life. I had to sacrifice a lot of time and dedicated hours searching And figuring out what it was that would fit what I was looking for. As I was trying to find what it was that I was going to be doing. I asked around from friends to family and even going around to different work- force centers to try and find what it was that would fit what I was looking for. After going around for a few weeks. I ended up coming to a decision after taking to one of my childhood friends that had been in business for awhile. Which he learned how to operate from his parents. After having a few conversations with my friend about the financial part of the business and speaking on how much profit you can make a month and making sure a certain amount of income a month that would guaranteed. That really caught my attention because that's what I was looking for. It wasn't the job description I was looking for because whatever it was that I had to be done I was willing to give it a chance. On top of that it all fell back on owning your own business to make this type on a income. So that was a start for what I was looking for. Since this was a lead way for what I was looking for I started to set my self myself up to start getting information on the job description to see if any of this was something I was really Wanted to put time into. Even tho everything sounded good I still needed to know for myself If this was what I was really looking for. Testing myself to see if I wanted to deal with this type of change in life to change the financial situation I was in. I set up a day with my friend Jojo which was already into the trucking industry and he was fully independent owner operator that traveled through the 48 states. I knew it was a lot for me to learn when it came to this industry to learn how to make the income I was looking to make. So we set up a date to hook up and roll out together to see even if this was something I was up too. We set up that date and stuck to it we both decided that it was best if I made a trip together with him from the west to the east coast to see if I was ready to jump into this industry to make a change for me and my family. We set that date and took off from California to Atlanta for a life changing trip with me not knowing nothing about this new change it was pretty cool that I had someone to give me a hand on walking me threw an over the road experience to even see if this was going to be my life changing experience that I was looking for. In this book we will find the secrets of happiness for men and women who want to make a change in their life who want to be happy and financial stable to make ends meet when, "you don't have a college degree or some type of certification. No matter what you been threw in life this is a opportunity that can change your life forever.

IF YOU'RE LIKE ME, AND want to find a way to support your yourself and your family financially. This book will give you an idea on how to find yourself. But let's face it, Life is tough and the easy

way only works for a little while. The book your holding is part of a unique nationwide plan to encourage as many women and men in their quests, to join the trucking industry to help them save them time and money in the long run. Khafra brang TruckDriverCoach.com to an existence to help individuals one by one to jump Start their career into the trucking industry and to never hesitate in how you feel on attacking the things you want to do in life. My sincere desire is that you will find fresh ideas and a new beginning with yourself in these pages. I'm hoping you will find the abundant life you're looking for.

Khafra Akbar
Founder & CEO

A coaching service helping Men-Women and families find their purpose in life threw the Trucking Industry.

P.S After reading this book, please pass it on to a friend or someone you think wants to join the, Trucking Industry.

MOVING TO CITY OF COMPTON in the late 80s grown-ing up around that time gang violence was high it was hard for a young black man to really pay attention in school due to the violence it was really hard to pay attention in school I found myself interested mostly learning in the field with hands-on training hanging out with a few different neighbors in different fields and construction and a lot of work done on ranch In my younger adult years I started getting into horseback riding with me and my mother and my kids we organized a horse program called the Compton Junior Posse which is now called the Compton cowboys everyone grew up and are officially cowboys and cow- girls which where the Compton cowboys my mother turned the program over to My ken folks enjoying myself being part of the program with me having kids at such a young age force me to recover to become more fi- nancially stable so I journeyed off looking to be more financially stable as I journey out into being an entrepreneur early on from opening up clothing store to construction to finding myself looking for a more secure financial stability which I found myself joining the trucking industry being an en- trepreneur always force myself into being an owner in the things that I got into so my mindset was a little different from the average always being a motivational person with me joining the Trucking industry not knowing I will be motivating others to join.

I N LIFE IT'S A TIME when you decIded to make a change In lIfe. ThIs may be a hard tIme you're havIng In lIfe when It seems lIke nothIng's goIng rIght or when you get to thInkIng about dIfferent sItuatIons maybe Income or you're just tryIng to fInd somethIng dIfferent to do wIth your lIfe. My reason for makIng changes and jumpIng Into the truckIng Industry was surprIsIng to myself because when I was young kid growIng up I never saId I wanted to be a trucker or a coach. But re- maInIng passIonate wIth a bIg heart for helpIng others changed my way of thInkIng make a certaIn amount of Income a month wIthout workIng for someone else. So whIle Going threw thIs stage I would be really talkIng to everybody around me tryIng to get some type of lead to hIgh- lIght somethIng that mIght grab my attentIon, to get me goIng. Also so I dIdn't have to worry If I was gonna be able to pay all my bIlls not know- Ing If you were gonna be able to pay your bIlls or not Is really not a good feelIng at all. It was always a sayIng In my head It's got to be a better way to survIve. I've always been an entrepreneur just about my whole lIfe when I was 18 years old I ran a handyman's busIness called the handyman specIalIst. We dId full bathroom kItchen remodelIng to stuckole to elec- trIcal work we provIded a lot of servIces that brought In a lot of calls for work. But of course It dIdn't start of that way of course thIngs was slow at the start. When beIng young black and In busIness for yourself there was a lot more you had to deal wIth when everyone Is almost lookIng at your lIke your tryIng to get over on them so I had to be able to learn how to sell my servIces whIle all thIs was happenIng. ThIs was a lot I saw that I had to deal wIth to make an Income but of course I had to start off somewhere so I had went and got some busIness cards prInted up had ordered some magnetIc sIgns to put on the sIde of my work trucks. I re- member at the tIme I had an astro van and a dodge cargo van that I was usIng for work trucks. ThIs two trucks were to haul whatever supplIes I needed to work on and whatever project I needed wIthout making a bunch of runs back and forth to the store for supplIes. Always obsessed wIth what I do. I Had found a passIon when I had an Idea to make some- thIng out of nothIng and be successful really opens your mInd to how you can really mold a successful Idea Into reallty. The Idea of beIng your own boss I loved It always fIgurIng out a way to make an Income wIthout workIng so hard Is a real blessIng. WIth always tryIng to grow In busIness I jumped Into retaIl wholesalIng thIngs. I opened up a clothIng store. I hIred someone to work In the store and stIll dId my handyman work. Handyman work was ok I advertIse In the pennysaver and If you knew how to cover your zones your phone would rIng all day It would keep you busy but the Income would be dIfferent just about every month whIch was the reason why I was lookIng Into dIfferent Investments. WhIch lead me to sellIng retaIl. Days I had a few jobs lIned up and had workers on the sIght I would go out Into the fashIon dIstrIct and would go fInd Items that I new and thought I could sale. GrowIng up In the cIty of compton you are aware about the aeras your In because of all the street vIolence that was every were. So I decIded to open a store but I wanted to be In a area where I would have mutual people comIng through. I ended up openIng a clothIng store In, Apple valley CalIfornIa. ThIs was up off the 15 fwy thIs beIng up In the mountaIns and the type of Items I was sellIng was hIp so I named the store stunazpeak clothIng. By the type of Items I was sellIng people would buy and say there gettIng there "stunt "on they need to get there" shIne "on "blIng blIng "so Stunnaz was for the hIp Items I sold and peak was for top of the mountaIns so that's where stunaz- peak came from and got put together now havIng a store takes dIfferent type of responsIbIllItIes wIthout a grantee amount of Income a month or at least close numbers to what I'm lookIng for stIll always lookIng for somethIng to Invest In after a couple of year after a whIle I notIce these stores Dd's dIscount started poppIng everywhere. I started to stop by these stores to check them out to see what they had (ThIs Is checkIng your competItors Items)because other clothes stores were my competItIon. I would try and stay updated wIth what was sellIng around me whIle I was In thIs busIness. I start to notIce they start to have some of the same Items I had so thIs was a very good thIng I dId to check my competItors prIces. sInce they had some of the Items I had I made sure I trIed to pIck up a lot of dIfferent Item they dIdn't have. Now I have lIttle more com- petItIon goIng but It dIdn't stop me from stayIng creatIve wIth pIckIng out the retaIl Iteams. As I notIced how the retaIl wave was when In retaIl wIth the flow of sales. DurIng the dIfferent holIdays made me keep In mInd the reasons for me InvestIng. Was to see what kInd of return I was gonna get. I knew a lot depended on advertIsIng but somethIng In my mInd was sayIng to myself that maybe I should try somethIng else. My mInd stIll open to others Ideas as I try to stay creatIve In busIness to keep a consIstent Income to support my famIly so we could enjoy some famIly tIme. But I new It was somethIng else that could make me more money. I just had to come across the rIght thIng. I really started thinking that I was gone be making a real bIg change with busIness. I started to ask around and talkIng to dIfferent people from our small cIty meetIngs. One day stoppIng by my mother's house I ran Into a old frIend. We started talkIng after we dIscussed some Issues I had and was goIng thru he started tellIng me about. What he had goIng on and Would offer to show me a lIttle of what he goes thru to make ends meet for hIm If I was Interested. After he ran by a lot stuff by me he. Then he ask me do you thInk you can handle thIs type of stuff. I saId I don't know but I'm wIllIng to try and see If I can. Or to see If I would lIke to even drIve trucks, Never thought about drIven trucks. But when you get to thInkIng about the Income you can make and need to make so you start to try and see If any of thIs truckIng stuff wIll work for me, for what I was lookIng for espe- cIally If It's gonna help me out. So we kept In contact after that he let me know on hIs next trIp to atlanta georgIa from calIfornIa he would let me know so I could rIde wIth hIm so I can see If I can't even handle thIs lIfestyle and Income But I knew I was all in for it. It kInda happened quIcker than I thought It was no later than a week later that he let me know that the trIp was In a few days so have my bags ready because we're goIng to be gone for a week and a half. So got my stuff ready so happy to see how thIs new thIng wIth truckIng can do for me and my famIly I was so happy to tell my gIrl and my kIds about It when It was tIme for hIm to come pIck me up. WHen he arrived he saw my kIds and gIrl there, he responded looks lIke It's a goIng away party. Just happy to do somethIng dIfferent In a posItIve way to help my famIly out more than I can now. I can remember that day lIke yesterday because that trIp changed my lIfe and had me lookIng In a total dIfferent dIrectIon. It all started from that very trIp calIfornIa to atlanta georgIa. he pIcked up the load In northern calIfornIa then came down pIcked me up then we headed out. I was askIng questIons but beIng new to thIs whole thIng I dIdn't know all the approprIate questIon but I asked the ones that came to my mInd. He let me know when he got loaded and when he had checked In wIth the broker to get a fuel advance. I'm lIke what that he says a advance on the load rate we negotIated they gIve you a certaIn amount of the load when you pIck up. I'm lIke ok I fIgured that was kInd of cool but dIdn't really under- stand it at the tIme but I'm takIn notes. Well I'm just sIttIng up sIghtsee- Ing the whole tIme just lIke a bIg kId fallIng asleep In the passenger seat every tIme he saId man gone head and lay It done I'm lIke I'm cool just sIttIng up just to see how long I can take It. thIs was a three or four day trIp he saId so I'm just tryIng to enjoy the trIp and suck up as much as possIble to take wIth me. knowIng we were goIng be drIvIng straIght tell he had tIme to break just knowing ahead of tIme made It not a problem for me at least not yet rIght, at least that's what I was tellIng myself. We had fueled up shortly after he pIcked me up whIch I never payed attentIon how long a truck can drIve before havIng to stop and get fuel agaIn. By the second tIme we stopped It was tIme for hIm to take a break to get ready to contInue the trip so we stop at a truck stop were he saId he lIke to take hIs breaks at. we pulled up to the pump he says were gonna fuel up fIrst then we'll take a shower when you purchase a certaIn amount of fuel they gIve you a free shower If you don't fuel at least 50 gallons then you have to pay $15.00 for a shower. thIs was a new truck stop experIence. I never knew you could stop at a truck stop to take a shower. They gIve you fresh towels If you don't have your own I thought that was pretty cool If you used It to your advantage whIle on the road so we freshened In up and headed back to the truck to get some rest. I remember that fIrst nIght beIng fresh up In the truck I showed up and got up on the bunk tIred just from sIttIng up all day so I feal rIght to sleep. We got up after our 10 hour break went to the restroom wash my face and brush my teeth then. We headed back down the road we drove for a lIttle bit by hIm knowIng the hIghway he already knew were to stop and get somethIng to eat from. He let me know that a food spot was comIng up that we were gonna stop at to grab a bIte to eat and take a lIttle break and then head back down the road I'm lIke cool let's eat I'm starvIng lIke marvIn. We pulled Into another truck stop I'm sayIng to myself now these truck stops be booming. We stopped got us somethIng to eat got full then headed back to the truck to rest our stomach for a mInute then he pulled of to headed down the road. The next couple of days dIdn't even seem to take that long to get us to the drop. we must of got there about three or four In the mornIng to delIver the load. we got there before thIs place opened up that day so we just kIcked back took a quIck nape tell they opened up for us to check In so we could get unloaded. In good tImIng you would thInk, rIght sInce we got there before they opened up, so we checked In when they opened up and my fIrst tIme experIenced to have a long waIt gettIng unloaded. I notIced that but dIdn't bother me at the tIme for one I knew I was stIll tIred but sInce I was" new" to thIs whole thIng I was In for the rIde. After we got unloaded we headed out to head to mIssIssIppI As We headed down the road from ATL It was nIght on the way In but on the way out the sun was coming up and and I tell you from seeIng all the dIfferent color leafs on the trees thIs tIme of the year was so beautIful to see. You'll Have to see it In your own eyes, Instead of In the books or In a calendars. Because In CalIfornIa the trees don't change these many colors the way they do out thIs way on the east coast. When we got there on our way to check In to the off Ice to bIll the brokers for the load pIcked up in California the brokers payed him his check for the load we just dropped. Then pIcked up the new paperwork for the load We had to pIck up to take back to calIfornIa. We weren't there that long of a tIme after we pIck up the paperwork we rolled out to the chIcken ranch whIch wasn't that for from where we were goIng. To pIck up a load of fresh chIcken that was my fIrst tIme goIng to a chIcken ranch. Where they provIde the chIcken that we see In our grocerIes storIes. ThIs was really crazy to me beIng at a chIcken ranch hands on for the fIrst tIme can be a real turn off. FIrst of all this place stInks lIke the walkIng dead second of all the place Is way back down some dark road that looks lIke somethIng wIld mIght jump out to feast off you. I'm lIke damn they're Is a busIness way back here shure knof follow the long dark dIrt road. when you get to the back, you can see where It's all goIng down at. You can see them brIng In the chIckens In on the trucks lIve watch them get unloaded them from one sIde run them thru the factory then all you see Is dead chIckens boxed up gettIng loaded up Into tractor traIlers seeIng thIs for the fIrst tIme was kInd of gross for real. The place stIck and you get to see how fresh the chIcken Is I guess when you don't see the process It doesn't bother you that much but when you see a whole lot of thIngs, ThIngs can change the way you feel about chIcken. As we were waItIng I was just thInkIng of how much money my frIend just made just by drIvIng and droppIng of a load. But I knew you had to own your own truck and traIler to make that much amount of Income. Just by hIm makIng that much amount of money In that short of a tIme, I really thought that was great. Then we were pIcking up another load to make more money on the way back. At that tIme I dIdn't know that you had optIons to take loads both ways, any how I thought that was really awesome not knowIng "nothIng", about truckIng when him showing me these type of numbers you can make weekly had my eyes open then he let me see the balance of what he made from the load we dropped off In Atlanta Ga. Man If I told you my thoughts after he let me know what the balance was that they just gave hIm for the load we just dropped the check he had got It was really ImpressIve. That was really motIvatIng when I seen that amount of an Income he just made In a few days thInkIng to myself "What I dId notIce buy the tIme we got to the chIcken ranch and buy the tIme we left the ranch that we were there waItIng to get loaded for more than ten hours are so whIch was cool because he saId we had to do a reset before headed back to CalIfornIa. Didn't know what that meant at the time but ok Also I got to learn the dIfference between a dry van traIler and a reefer traIler. Once we had to set the temperature on the traIler. I dIdn't know If that was regular or what but all I knew that I was down for whatever. To see even If I could handle all thIs. After sIttIng there for a nIce long tIme I do remember then they called us to a door so that they can start loadIng our load up to take back to callfornIa. So we pulled around to back up to the dock to get loaded up whIch took probably 8 or so more hours or more. ThIs Is when he lets me know that you have to do a 34 hour reset once you cover so many hours In a workweek thIs Is one of the rules you have to follow when beIng a truckIng. You have to have all your paper- work rIght so when the hIghway patrols pull you over you'll be already ready for whatever they're goIng to ask you for because drIvIng these trucks you wIll get pull over at some poInt In tIme and If your paperwork Is not rIght you wIll be receIvIng a fIne that you do not want or even can be placed out of servIce dependIng on what's wrong on your log book. GettIng put out of servIce can jeopardIze a lot when tryIng to be on tIme for your delIvery and the next day to come. So thIs Is a must learn when you reach the drIver seat of the truck if your not on e logs ELB. As we stIll waIted for them to fInIsh loadIng or load up we both layed down back Into the sleeper of the truck. By the way he had a 2005 kenwood double bunk 10 speed. Few hours later they let us know that we were loaded up and that we were ready to roll out.

He Went back Into the offIce to sIgn the paperwork, thIs Is to confIrm the load and that we just pIcked up. ThIs Is proof of Inventory of the load. When delIverIng theIr product thIs Is part of shIppIng and receIvIng. They gIve you a shIppIng manIfest to let you know what product Is beIng transported In your traIler. So he gets back to the truck starts It up we pull forward to lock the load In wIth load locks shut the doors and lock them then pulled away from the door so the next truck can back In proceed wIth a safety check. He wanted me to pay attention to just to keep me Informed and of thIs procedure checkIng the tIre all lIghts, blInkers, wIndshIeld wIpers, and If water sprays the wIndshIeld, fIre extInguIsher emergency reflectors, any aIr leaks or worker leaks or oIl make sure the belts are In good condItIon not to lose or to tIght make Sure your defroster Is workIng properly. You would commIt to repeatIng these steps throughout the day and when stoppIng at the truck stops to keep you a lot more safer on the road. Safety plays a super bIg part of our success when out here on the road. LIttle thIngs If you pay attention to when out here on the road can save you bIg buck$$$$. So you need to really pay attentIon to your truck that your operatIng when out on

the road pay real close statIon to every noIse It make to how It deals
when rollIng down the hIghway. also check the log book or ELB make
sure that It's rIght. As I thought to myself so far so good to see how
thIngs operate hands on, for myself In thIs way doesn't seem to be,
really that dIffIcult to operate thIs truck or go Into busIness I really
wanted to make a change In my lIfe. We fInIshed that safety check on
the truck and traIler. I knew It was a lot more to It and I knew It would
be a rough tIme when out on the road specIally when not knowIng
how to handle thIngs when they went wrong but I was all In for the
rIde especIally as bad as I wanted to do somethIng else to make an
Income and these numbers I saw, your not makIng thIs at no regular
job so I sucked everythIng up that I could he have to offer because. I
Knew It wouldn't be too many other people to let me do what he was
lettIng me do at thIs tIme when I was lookIng for a change. Even tho
I couldn't drIve or operate the truck I knew If I put my mInd to It.
That I wIll make some- thIng happen. After gettIng loaded up and he
went to receIve the paper- work for the load. We headed out down the
road. He let me know It won't be that long before we get to the truck
stop they have a restaurant InsIde there so we'll stop go InsIde after
fuelIng and grab us a bIte to eat so we dId just that. When we got In
sIde we both ordered steak and eggs and oranges juIce. It was pretty
tasty we fInIshed up and headed back to the truck rested our stomps
for a mIn then we headed out back down the road. He also let me
know when you're on a certaIn rougt that you wIll fInd out where the
good food Is at EspecIally when you start gettIng burnt out on all the
food they wIll have for you at theses truck stops. But I tell you thIs, the
flyIng J be havIng some good hot plate meals. I wana say the food Is
somethIng lIke denny's. They had mash potatoes green beans meatloaf
mac and cheese baked chIcken and corn. When beIng In a rush and
that beIng ready to go made It real convenIent and tIme savIng. On
The way back he saId he saId we was goIng to stop at thIs bbq joInt
he saId every tIme he came thIs way thIs Is a must stop. So yes after a
few hours we ended up at the bbq joInt. So we went In to dIne In
whIle on our break. As I ordered my food lookIng at the meat as they
slIced It to put It on my plate and the way the meat was comIng threw
the meat machIne to make the beef sandwIch was lookIng so delIcIous.
When tastIng the food you really can tell the dIfference between the

food In CalIfornIa and out of state. The food was so bomb that I had to take a order to go for the road for latter. So knowIng your route and the food stops really brIng lIfe back In too you whIle on the road so seconds It was before we headed out back down the road. So far so good all thIs truckIng stuff dIdn't seem so bad even tho I knew I haven't seen half of It but I saId to myself I thInk I found my new occupatIon I saId to myself I thInk I can make thIs work. Now my frIend dIdn't work for a company he owned hIs own hIs truck and hIs 48 foot spread axle reefer traIler. Yes he was hIs own boss and he dIdn't have to check In wIth anybody but the broker of the load. That was pretty cool. Also dependIng on how you wanna get started sInce your so thrIlled to gettIng goIng can be kInda expensIve. But I dIdn't worry about that I just knew I needed to do somethIng to change wIth consIstency and a certaIn amount of Income monthly. I knew that I had to try somethIng else. WIth the confIdence I had to do what I needed to get rollen. He drove for hIs hours he could then we pulled on It to a truck stop to get some rest. He kept tellIng me about you had to log your hours In the logbook that part at that tIme just was a lIttle confusIng to myself but I knew when that tIme came I would be ready to attack It to learn what I needed. Seems lIke ever sInce we left CalIfornIa every state been lIke 100 degrees it was sum- mer time so the hot weather is different from California. I'm tellIng you, TIll you ever leave CalIfornIa to experIence the weather In another state or If you have. You'll never understand, He let me know on our way back we have two drops Instead of one on our way back to CalIfornIa one In San DIego CalIfornIa and the other one El Monte CalIfornIa. we started our day as he was still teaching e know a lIttle more about the log book sayIng you have a 14 hour work day but you can work 11 hour out the day and the other hours have to be documented to show you took your breaks and fuelIng tImIng. After our work day we stop at a dIfferent truck stop to shower and up. Its a trip to stop and see things for the fIrst tIme at thIs these different truck stops to see how nIce they can be I mean we stopped at one but thIs one whIch I notIced It was called the loves they have the best showers to me there are a few different truck stops out there on the road to fInd that other truck stops had them also but I lIked the loves 💙 the best, that was my opInIon. I thought It was pretty cool to stop at the dIfferent truck stops so you can see the dIfference In they way they servIce you, whIch ones had the hot food ready to go when you weren't tryIng to waste that much tIme and what each one dIdn't have everythIng you want As you try to not spend that much tIme In the truck stop especIally when you know you have a long stretch on the hIghway to burn up. As they say hammer down. DrIvIng thru the dIfferent states I notIced that you had to pass dIfferent scales when enterIng another state he says you're supposed to pull Into the scales when enterIng and leavIng the state unless you have prepass equIpped wIth your truck and It gIves you the green lIght. But if not you have to enter the scales were they do proper searchIng of the truck for safety reasons if your Dot and Mc number are not up to date will safety inspections etc. You get a red lIght If you have multIple cItatIons from your company for not beIng In complIne of servIce to your truck thIs wIll gIve you poInts on your authority so if your points go up. To certain levels you wIll start gettIng pulled Into the scales throughout the states so you have to know these thIs to be successful In truckIng because thIs wIll happen untIl your scores goes down ThIs Is how they keep up wIth safety. Safety plays a huge part In truckIng. He had pre pass so we basIcally just drove straIght to Atlanta then back to CalIfornIa by passIng the scales do to keeping the truck up with his mantanis and clean and safe So whIle everybody was In lIne waItIng to cross we just drove rIght on thru. I told myself I defInItely need one of those when I get rollen. We made good tImIng to CalIfornIa We dropped the fIrst load early In the mornIng It was almost noon when we got to the second drop. I asked hIm where do you take the papers to to get paId. He saId he had to maIl them off when they receIve the paperwork and check It then they wIll cut and maIl out a check wIth the balance. We left on a tuesday and was back the followIng thursday. A week or so for some good Income yea It was a nIce rIde for a nIce check Is what I was thInkIng. As we headed back to the cIty to drop me off he says so what you thInk about truckIng now I had to let hIm know that I wIll be joInIng thIs truckIng famIly from my experIence from thIs trIp It dIdn't take me long for me to make my decIsIon about what I wanted to do WIth the drIllIng runnIng threw me sayIng to myself that thIs Is what I wanted to do soon as I got back I started searchIng for dIf- ferent schools and. I'll gIve you an update Let me get out here and make somethIng happen so I can let you know that I'm really serIous. Man I have to fInd me a truckIng school he dropped me off I was so pumped up just already seeIng myself goIng thru the process and It haven't even started yet. I Was so excIted It was lIke thIs feelIng I got when I saId to myself yes thIs Is what I need wIth no doubt In my mInd I went out soon as I got back to get Into a trucking school so I Can Get my cdls. Once I put my mInd to that. That's really all I dId was research and fInd whIch one was goIng to work for me. As I dId my research about dIfferent schools they had In the area and read the revIews and just kept lookIng for one tIll. I came across one that I seen that can work wIth when and how I wanted thIngs to work for me. I got rIght on It and sIgned up and started rIght away. KnowIng I needed the traInIng to take me to the next level (key traInIng to take me to the next level) So I started lookIng up the dIfference between the bIg companIes and small ones as I was lookIng up the dIffer- ence I found out was the prIce fIrst of all was a bIg dIfference wIth the qualIfIcatIon you needed was a bIg dIfference. The bIg companIes had fundIng to where you can receIve your CDL's threw them and If you drove for them for a year you dIdn't have to pay for your cdl's and drIve for them for two year and they wIll reImburse you the 4k or 5k there are chargIng you for your cdl's this process can change over time but then I found out that the smaller truckIng schools had a cheaper prIce and they wIll traIn you to pass the test to get your cdls. By me already knowIng where I was tryIng to get goIng to a bIg company wasn't what I was lookIng for. I was just tryIng to get my cdls so I can learn to drIve and go out and get my own truck and start my own company goIng Independent I knew what I wanted. I just had to fIgure It out whIch way was gonna work for me. After lookIng the dIfferent truckIng schools up I decIded to go wIth a small truckIng school called professIonal truck drIvIng school It was In Los angeles ca I Had paId cash for thIs course they had a pay tIll you pass course and they had a short course for 1000.00 they'll traIn you a certaIn amount of hours and a couple tImes to the dmv to take the test and If you dIdn't pass In that tImIng you had to pay agaIn. DoIng research on how much thIngs were gonna cost for me to get to get started I just paId the traIn tell pass course for 1600.00. That meant however many tImes to the dmv In there truck. I couldn't waIt to get up to the school to sIgn up I called up to the school to make sure when I could start so I dIdn't get up there for nothIng. I got a tIme and a date to meet at the school to sIgn up. I was so excIted of the decIsIons I was makIng I just felt It was the rIght thIng to do I couldn't waIt to get down there to see how thIngs were goIng to go. When I got there the owner was there I guess he was the one that was sIgnIng everybody up wIth the dIfferent courses. As we Induced ourselves he let me know the way he handles hIs classes. You sIgn up then he'll supply you wIth materIals to study whIch were three dIfferent test and there were three of each they all had the same questIons but asked them dIfferent ways the three test covered general knowledge-combInatIon-and aIr brakes so I would have to study these materIals before I start the behInd the wheel traInIng also then enter a drug and physIcal program that's part of holdIng a CDL. Then when you get to the dmv you have to pay a $50.00 fee to take the test once you pass the test to receIve your permIt then you can start your behInd the wheel traInIng to complete the testIng to receIve your cdl's. Once you get your permIt he has a dvd of an In cab and out cab InspectIon of the truck to study before proceedIng to the next step wIth hIm. lettIng me know wIth practIcIng a couple hours a day depend- Ing on what days and hours he had avaIlable on hIs calendar. As we over- looked the calendar to see what days were avaIlable for me to choose from. But once I get my permIt I wIll be able to choose the dates to start the behInd the wheel traInIng. ThIs was lIke beIng back In school but what I dId notIce you have to pay for knowledge to stay more In control of your future. So I purchased the dvd because I had to purchase It separately and receIved my materIals for studyIng. After gettIng ready to pay the class he had let me know that you could pay In payments as you attended but have to be paId In full before takIng you to the dmv for testIng In the truck to receive your cdls. So you had optIons to pay In full or pay payments. I was all In I sIgned the agreement of enrollIng and payed to start my course. Not knowIng how long thIs was goIng to take me to furnIsh the course It dIdn't bother me because I knew I was not fIxn to play any games about this I study as much as possIble. I was so commItted to make a change thIs was fuel to my soul It felt lIke. After sIgnIng up and settIng my sched-ule I couldn't waIt to get to the house to start studyIng. BeIng so deter-mIned wIth my studyIng. My brother would pop up and say wasn't you just studyIng earlIer when we talked to me. I replIed sure was thIs the only way. I'm Gonna pass In good tImIng wIthout faIlIng and wastIng tIme. WIth me really commIttIng to change I had to be head In I don't need no chIll tIme just to study.

So determIned thats what I dId I studIed the dvd and that three test lIke If I was taken fInales In school. I studIed everyday most of the tIme when I wasn't to bIzzy. I started spendIng most of the days studyIng and slowed down on my project. But I knew It would all work out. I Was RaIsed up rIdIng horses and pullIng horse traIlers In the cIty of compton so when It came to the behInd the wheel traInIng I knew It was gonna be a lIttle more easIer for me. It dIdn't take long at all for me to get my permIt wIth all the hard studyIng I was doIng It was about a whole month before I went down to go and take my test to get my permIt. So happy wIth myself of what I was doIng. When I got around my frIends I let them In on what I was up too I had checked Into truckIng school and gettIng ready to be a professIonal truck drIver. Word got around to a couple more of my frIends that was In the truckIng Industry had caught up to me and let me know that hIs company Is gonna be ready for another drIver shortly we're just waiting for them to fInIsh up wIth the truck If you get your hard card In tIme I could pull you In. I know you're In traInIng but when you pass let me know so I can get u In just have your pops rIde wIth you to make sure your good and I'll get you the job. I couldn't belIeve what I was hear-Ing. So I say are you serIous he says man just call me when I get my cdls and Im let the boss know to put u up In the truck. I was just gettIng started and had a job I can jump too soon as I'm done wIth traInIng. ThInkIng let's just stay In full motIon Is all I can thInk of. That's cool how all that fell through because all the research I had done that It was gonna be dIf- fIcult to get a job from what I have been lookIng Into and at from lookIng thIngs up on lIne. By hIm gIvIng me the opportunIty to put me In that posItIon I was so excIted. The whole tIme In school that made me want to study even more to hurry up so I can pass the testIng to get to work. KnowIng that I was really studIng my but off tIll It was tIme to take the test. I couldn't waIt to get to the poInt to take the test. I remembered I stayed up late studyIng the nIght before then got up early the next day went over my notes got somethIng to eat and headed up there to take the test It was a small waIt tIll It was my turn for my In-cab/out- cab InspectIon. ThIs Is the fIrst test you do before the truck and traIler. So happy and excIted to take the test I put my studyIng In I just knew I was goIng to pass. It was my turn I approached the truck checked for leaks under the truck and make sure everythIng was In good workIng condItIons make sure the belts went to lose or to tIght. Before I got Into the truck for my Incab InspectIon. Soon as I got up In the truck I don't know what hap- pened but seems lIke my mInd went blank I couldn't thInk of anythIng. So excIted to take the test that I got shocked and now becomIng a lIttle frustrated the Instructor gave me a lIttle more tIme to commIt but too late I blanked out and faIled the test. DIsappoInted In myself I had to make sure that that was not gonna happen agaIn. After chicken back In to see how the schedule was lookIng lIke to pIck me another day to retake the test the next avaIlable date wasn't for a whole month. I couldn't do nothIng about that so I just study more and more and thIs wasn't gonna be the reason when I go back to take the test agaIn. wIth me goIng over and over the dvd to the test and studyIng I dId. It seemed lIke the longest 30 days ever seems lIke when you waItIng on a date seems lIke the days start goIng slower. Soon as that day came I was so excited but I was so ready not really that excIted but comfortable, now it's about applyIng myself to what I was learnIng. That day everythIng was just so smooth I ran threw the test lIke flyIng colors then we proceed to ally dockIng to the parallel parkIng han- dled that wIth no problem. I had a female Instructor she was always smIl- Ing that made thIngs kInd of easter also let me know I wasn't doIng to bad to that I scared her well at least that's what I thought tIll we headed out for the over the road traInIng. I followed the roughy she poInted out that Is all she pretty much saId whIle In the truck I dIdn't know what she was thInkIng In my head. Then she says next tIme I stop at the stop lIght make sure you leave at least two feet In front of you between the truck and the sIdewalk lIne. Put I pass...I was so happy that day. I knew I was gonna have a good year that year. I gave her a hIgh fIve and waIted for my prInt out. WaItIng wIth the bIggest smIle on my face I couldn't waIt to get home to tell my kIds and my gIrl that I passed and Is on my way to the money. RIght after I called my frIend to let hIm know I passed the test. He saId I'm sure fIxn to let the boss know. So get ready to go down the road on the next load or so. Let your pops know so he can also be ready. Now waItIng on my hard copy to come In the mail they say the waIt Is 4 to 6 weeks to receIve. so whIle I'm just adjustIng for the waIt for my hard copy to come In the maIl a week passed by I was just checking the maIl as usually to fInd out I had some maIl and ended up beIng my hard copy In the maIl, smIlIng hard sayIng It's only been a week and It's here man I tell you the way I was feelIng I called my frIend and let hIm know I had my hard copy had came he was lIke cool and that was fast I'm lIke rIght. Fast as I'm tryIng to get to the money seems lIke someone feels the power In my movement. My frIend called me rIght and saId the boss saId can you come down and fIll out the job applIcatIon and brIng my Id so he can send a copy to the Insurance company to see about gettIng me added on as a drIver. When I got to the yard just to go and sIgn the applIcatIon and to get ran by the Insurance company It must dIdn't take that long as I was there he asked me If I was ready to roll out and I'm lIke what roll out rIght now he's lIke yea the truck Is sItt Bg really got over there the trucks me your grandson man be drIvIng. He saId I can head out now or waIt tIll In the mornIng? I asked hIm to gIve me a mInute as I stepped outsIde. And what was so crazy my pops came by just to check on the process that I was In to see when we were rollIng out. I told hIm I'll let hIm know somethIng thIs evenIng and he was stIll waItIng on me to call. My pops had came by before the maIlman ran so he dIdn't know that my hard copy came tIll I had gave hIm a call when I stepped out of the offIce soon as he ask me to roll out. I called my pops and let hIm know my hard card had come after he left earlIer and I called In to check the status wIth the job when the boss got on the phone he asked me to come up In to sIgn the applIcatIon so I can get added on to the Insurance company as a drIver. Soon as they gave hIm a update as me beIng the drIver he asked me. Am I ready to roll out tonIght or In the mornIng. So I had to call you back wIth an update wIth the progress so here It Is so are we leavIng tonIght or In the mornIng. Pops let me know that we should leave to nIght so we can start our day fresh at a pIc In the mornIng I'm ok cool let me let hIm know. As I stepped back Into the offIce to let hIm know what I decIded. That I wIll come back to load my stuff up and we'll leave tonIght so I'm take off to grab my stuff cuz I defInItely dId thInk I was rollIng out as I came In to sIgn the job aplIcacIón. So I was To head out to grab my stuff and I'll be back In a couple of hours I rolled out back to the house so excIted. I had to call pops back to let hIm know we all good pops get cha bags ready and let's head out to the truck yard to get the truck to head out pops Is lIke cool I'll see you at the yard cool see you In a few. As I got to the yard my pops was pullIng up at the same tIme as we parked to get our stuff loaded up In the truck. The boss had the truck started up and ready for us to roll out he says he just servIced the truck so all fluIds It topped off so just pay attentIon to the Gage's and you'll be alrIght. I'm thInkIng cool. Then I go Into the offIce to get my InformatIon I needed In pIckIng up the load and made sure I had all Paperwork and documents I needed for the truck and trailer then we got ready to hIt the road" jack "wIth me thInkIng to myself It's crazy how thIngs been goIng since I commItted myself to doIng thIs truckIng thIng and thInkIng In my mInd maybe thIs was meant for me to do after all seems lIke thIngs was flowIng smoothly lIke If this was It. Just thInkIng to myself how the day went, EarlIer that mornIng my father came by. Now we're headed up to SelIna's Ca to pIck up a load to head out to Atlanta GA. We had four pIcks and one drop pops saId see I told you let's start off tonIght so we can be fresh In the mornIng and ready to start our day cuz we got a long one. I'm cool you know I don't know nothIng I'm just taken notes. As we left the yard we had to make a quIck left turn down a long street. Now at thIs tIme my pops new I went to truckIng school to get my lIcense. He has hIs commercIal lIcense but he abstaIned hIs In another school some dIfferent type of truckIng school when they assIst hIm wIth a dIfferent type of traInIng dIfferent drIvIng practIces he had to do he saId he to do to obtaIn hIs lIcense. And by sIttIng up In thIs truck I notIced that thIs truck had all kInds of stuff that wasn't In the truck that I was traInIng In. Only because I had my father wIth me I waste so nervous but I was nervous as heck If you ask me. LookIng at all thIs InsIde the truck not knowIng nothIng I played It smooth off for pops and the boss. But at that moment I had to let hIm know I was lIke pops he was lIke was up champ he always called me champ. I'm lIke pops I need you to drIve. He looked at me and saId man you just started what do you mean we aInt even went four blocks. I'm lIke I know remember when I asked you If I got the job wIll you rIde wIth me and you happIly saId yes. He saId yes. It was because I knew that that I dIdn't know how to drIve thIs truck by myself by never beIng down the road before. I would be headed out to kIll someone wIthout knowIng how to drIve thIs truck better yet by myself. That's y I asked you to roll wIth me If you had the tIme because I knew you would be happy for me and would love to show me some trucker tIps I dIdn't know about. He was lIke man are you serIous, I'm lIke yea pops He saId alrIght pull over as we swItched seats and put or seat belts on. He saId you got too much jelly for the donut. Yea man you sure know how to fInger stuff out how you get a job and don't know how to drIve that's to smOoth for me but we rollin -HIm -Yea ....-Me -Yup. As we made our way out to our fIrst pIc we got there by mIdnIght and got us a parkIng spot to waIt to start our day wIth n the mornIng. On our way there my pops was explaInIng everythIng he was doIng to me so I can start understandIng how to operate thIs truck especIally when you get loaded up and carryIng 43,500.00 pounds of weIght In the traIler you need to know how to stay In control of your truck. As we laId out to get some rest to start our day tomorrow. The next day after we got up when the fIrst pIc opened up we talked and decided he would be doing the drIven and we decIded that he was goIng to drIve to do the pIcks and when we got ready to head back down to head over the great vIne he'll continue showing me a lot of tips i needed to know so I can start gettIng my over the road traIn- Ing as we proceeded. After gettIng loaded up. I just paId good attentIon whIle he would back up to the docs but then I would notice I could drIve between the pIcks to get more practIce In but dIdn't wanna waste that much tIme between loads to keep up wIth tImIng whIle we were pIckIng the pIcks up. BeIng new whIle drIvIng and tryIng to switch the gear in the truck Into hIgh gear It was stIll a lIttle complIcated. After notIcIng whIle we were drIvIng on flat land It wasn't so bad when tryIng to swItch gears wIth the approprIate rpms to make thIngs flow wIthout tearIng anythIng up on the truck was somethIng to learn. By me just learnIng, by the tIme we got to the second drop It was a lIttle late wIth the waItIng to get loaded and the drIve tIme to the next pIckup wIth them closIng early by It beIng the weekend. WIth the drIve tIme to the thIrd pIc we knew we wasn't gonna make It so we checked In at the second pIc got loaded up and drove to the thIrd pIc to start In the mornIng. As we made It to the thIrd pIc they were stIll open loadIng up other trucks as we checked In they let us know that they would be able to load us up we just had to waItIng tIll they called us to a door and they dIdn't know how long the waIt was gonna be, whIch was cool anyway because we stIll had to waIt tIll the am to pIck up the last pIc beIng a lIttle tIred from being nervous from drIvIng that day when I jumped In the back to rest a bIt I fell rIght out to wake up to see we were stIll waItIng to get loaded so I go back In to check In to see what was goIng on they saId that we stIll have to waIt to get loaded they wIll let us know so we couldn't do nothIng but waIt for them to call us. KnowIng that the last pIck closed early and by us gettIng here yesterday I knew we would be at the last drop early to roll out but dIdn't seem to go that way we sat there tIll about 10 clock the next day wIth having to drIve an hour and 45 mIn to the last pIc I was startIng to get a lIttle worrIed If we were gonna make It to the last pIc In time to get loaded the way thIngs were lookIng we were pressIng tIme and It looked lIke we were not goIng to make It by the tIme we made It to the door I knew we were gonna be there another day out to grab thIs last load. WhIch I dIdn't mInd I was just so happy to be drIvIng and to be wIth my pops wIth my fIrst job I got and he got to be my traIner never could ImagIne that, out the blue It really amazes me never knowIng thIs would fall all together thIs way but I loved every bIt of It My father dId also We fInally got a door to get loaded up and headed to the last pIc before we headed back down I 5 to go back over the when we got to the pic they didn't take long to load us up which was cool then we headed back down the road on the way to the grape vIne that's when I Got back behInd the wheel after watchIng hIm wIth that hIgh and low bUtton I fIgured It couldn't be too dIffIcult pops made It look so sImple so I took notes and followed through as I got us down the road all the way the the grapevIne. Me," I'm" lIke I got thIs as I started makIng my way up the hIll notIced that the truck started to slow down and you could now fIll that weIght that you have In the traIler and the truck pullIng the weIght by Itself, and pops lettIng me know what's goIng on and what I'm going to be needIng to do In a mIn once the truck slows down a lIttle more he let's me know I need to watch the rpms before downshIftIng. As he was lettIng me know to shIft so I down shIfted one gear then another gear and that's when It kIcked In and that's what they say when truckIng really starts. I was fIne tIll we hIt that hIll I dIdn't reallze wIth all that weIght that It would affect the way you shIft.' im sayIng to myself as much as I know how to drIve a stIck shIft and can burn out and do donuts thIs shouldn't be too dIffIcult. RIght as I started to try and downshIft wIth thInkIng how a car shIfts thInkIng I was goIng to apply the same actIon when swItchIng gears. But this hole way of shIftIng Is totally dIfferent whIch really got me, as I started up the hIll as the hill got steeper the truck started goIng slower and slower as I started to shIft the gears. I started scratchIng gears My pops started sayIng just make sure your hazardous are on. Soon as he said that Now I messed a gear and the truck just slowed down so much, thInkIng thIs works lIke a car I tell you I started scratching the heck out of them gears my pops started to let me know check your hazards make sure they're on and stop and let's hurry up and swItch seats so I can get us up the hIll my hands were sweatIng so bad and my arms were so tIght just from holding the steering wheel tight beIng so nervous we swItched seats real quIck. So he can take over I'm lIke cool now It's tIme for hIm to show me how thIs truckIng thIngs works and how your suppose to operate It to make It work for you so he got into the driving seat and got the truck back rollen slowly as we got up to about 25 mph he let me know that we were in the trucks clImbIng gear depended on the waIt In the traIler your clImbIng gear depends on the waIt you'll be pullIng, to determIne that gear when clImb- Ing. Pops would break down everythIng that he could to help me be a better drIver. He says don't rush when you feel the truck is starting to start pullIng and tryIng to get It into to gear and u missed the gear It's better to slow down stop and start over when it's safe if getting stuck this is one way you can get back on track just make sure your hazard are on and So stop and start over practIce that next go round and we'll see how that works for you. WIth my pops knowIng a lot about truckIng and beIng a drIver hImself that wIth no doubt In my mInd that I couldn't walk myself through these steps by myself and be successful. That's one of the real reasons I'm glad I could put thIs together to make It happen for me and get the traInIng from my father I needed to use when startIng to operate when startIng own busIness. So he drove us over the grapevIne then I took over once we got to the other sIde, he also had to show me how to come down a steep hIll grabe and explaIns how to fInd your gear to the speed your going and to use your engine breaks to slow yourself down with the weIght you'll be haulIng. BesIdes just readIng No, It's totally dIfferent beIng behInd the wheel and I was so glad he could brIng that to my at- tentIon because I know I would of messed somethIng up me beIng alone In the truck and not knowIng. He drove us all the way to chIchila Ca by the tIme we got there It was tIme for us to take a break so we showered up there and took It back to the truck to get some rest so we can head out. The next day. I took over the wheel from there for a second tIme to try and make It up the next hIll. I made It up some then I proceed lIke he told me to so when the truck started to slow all the way down and I couldn't figure out the next gear. I slowed down then stopped and started over whIch work perfectly when thIngs got a lIttle rough. but Pops made it look smooth to keep you In a flow that works for u when you're a lIttle nervous. As we came to a stop and he got us over that hIll and Into Az to mIle mark 100 then I took over from there sInce It was a long stretch of the hIghway for me to get some more mIles under my belt whIch Is y, I'm out here to suck thIs all up much as I can whIle I was wIth my pops for sure, buy thIs tIme we were needIng fuel, so I had to call In to talk to Angel to get a fuel ad- vance whIch Is what he ask me to do when the fuel got low I had know Idea of what It was or how It worked but I knew my pops dId so I just acted lIke I dId tIll I brought It to my father's attentIon pops we gettIng low on fuel I'm callIng Angil to get the fuel advance he's like ok cool so we can stay In motIon so we can stay In control of our free tIme on the hIghway case we wanna stop and extra hour or so somewhere where you wanna take a break. I'm lIke cool cuz I don't know nothIng about how to really take advantage of the clock so I'm lIke cool I call Angil up and let him know I needed a fuel advance and he saId cool he'll hIt me rIght back wIth a com check I'm lIke cool. We ended up pullIng up to a truck stop around mIle mark 200 to get fuel and to waIt for Angil to call back wIth the com check for the fuel. He took about 20 mIn to hIt me back wIth the com check We had just pulled up to the pump when he call'd back so It was lIke rIght on tIme. LettIng my pops know and he new I never used the com check before that he would come on In wIth me just to show me hands on how It works and let me know that It was a money code and they can send money to you In that form he saId you have to pay attentIon where you stop because some truck stops don't take the com check if you have to it's safer to pull over And call and check if they take it then to get off your rough because It can take some tIme to get back on rough. ThIs Is another lesIón that he taught wIthout wastIng a lot of tIme to something to know because I hated to waste tIme I would rather someone show me something hands on that's just the type of way I lIked to learn thIngs in my opinion for me to understand As we fueled up and and got ready to head back down the road wIth me drIvIng and beIng new to the truck shIftIng. I really had to get the way you shIft In a car out my head this Is totally dIfferent. WhIch made you really pay attentIon to way the truck sounds and even watchIng the rpms on the truck when you shIfted Is a way of lettIng you know when to shIft. AssumIng how to do somethIng can really put you In a bad sItuatIon If you're not aware of what you're doIng. BeIng a fast learner I felt that I would be able to learn thIs process and be a pro In no tIme but tellIng myself I know It wIll take a whIle may even take longer then I thought but I was all In for the rIde. After seeIng Hands on that It wasn't goIng to be as quIck as drIvIng a car but hey I'm In for the long run. We left the truck stop we were topped off and In for some hours down the road. As I was drIvIng down the road I notIced that we had a long straIght hIghway and as I would shIft gears I'm rolling down the hIghway from speedIng up to slowIng down I had to keep practIcIng down shIftIng and swItchIng gears at the approprIate rpms so I worked on that goIng down the hIghway the hIghway at the tIme it wasn't really that much traffIc so we was rollin all the way In to Tyson Az where we ended up stop at thIs truck stop called the TrIple T whIch had a restaurant and a huge parkIng lot to park so we went InSIde of course we had to go In and grab us somethIng to eat By that tIme we had already been drIvIng a whole work day so we decIded to go head and rest up there for the nIght till we decided to continue down the road. We dIdn't see a TA but there was one down the road so we decIded that we'll stop there tomorrow. To save money on taken a shower we fueled 50 gallons at the pilot. On our way Into New MexIco by now by pops says let's take a break at a truck ck stop comIng up I seen the sIgn say there's a couple comIng up and we seen there a T A comIng up TravIs centers of AmerIca Is the name of the truck stop he let me know thIs Is one of the truck stops he lIkes to stop at when he would be on the road. As we get closer to the exIt off the freeway I pulled In and pulled up to the fuel pump and stopped as everyone else dId smIl- Ing feelIng lIke a pro once I stop and put the truck In park. we headed Into the truck stop to pay for the fuel i let the assIstance know I had an express code from a com check to pay for the fuel she asked me If I had a ultra one card ?I responded what's Is an ultra one card. She says a card you can request to redeem your poInts every tIme you fuel over 50 gallons you'll receIve a free shower whIch I thought was really cool because show- ers cost $14.00 dollars at the truck stop so savIng money and adding poInts. I was all In for savIng money specIally to take It home especIally knowIng you was gonna be out on the road for some tIme and dIdn't know for how long so I asked where do I get one she saId I can get a temporary one tell the one they'll send me one In the maIl wIth my name on It. I'm lIke y'all sendIng these of lIke credIt cards but I'm lIke ok I got my tem- porary card paId for some more fuel and got our free shower poInts added to my temporary card so I won't have to pay for our shower tonIght we needed then to fInd out that you can use one shower tIcket to pay for two showers whIch was even much better hey thEse truck stops sure know how to get your money savIng on two shower 2 shower x2 =28 that mean It would be 28 dollars every tIme we went to take a shower. That was gonna add up so I wIll sure be usIng my card to gaIn my poInts to receIve my free shower poInts. At thIs tIme I went back to the truck to fuel up then went back In to get my receIpt for the fuel. To keep up wIth the gallons of fuel I bought. ThIs Is part of my job beIng a drIver to collect all the fuel receIpts and turn them In wIth all the Paperwork sIgned from the receIver from the loads we pIcked up and dropped off Into the offIce when we got back to keep on records. ThIs Is also what he saId Is a part of my job to gettIng paId so I had to stay on top of thIngs to make Sure I dId just that. So I headed back to the truck to head down the road. Pops lettIng me know you wanna save as much as possIble when you out here. He also saId when you're out here tryIng to make your money your wana have all your paperwork rIght obey all the traffIc laws and make sure you always check your truck and traIler because thIs we'll have you ready so when you get ready to get In your truck you wIll already know what to do and how to do It. Another thIng he saId you can be hard headed and not lIsten and do what you wanna do but one thIng you wIll learn to obey. Because you're either gonna go to work and pay yourself or your gonna go work for the man. I asked hIm what does he mean by that. When You're out here on the road and you're not obeyIng the laws and get sIghted a tIcket that means Now you have to work to pay the tIcket off. Because they wIll sus- pend your lIcense If you don't pay your tIcket or tIckets. So work to pay yourself or go to work to pay hIm. That's what he was sayIng so yea that's really a hIghlIght for the records. So whIle I'm out here I'll keep that In mInd whIle tryIng to get payed. Then he saId you need to suck all thIs up because you don't know how long thIs Is gonna last. I'm lIke what do you mean he says by me just gettIng my Cdls and gettIng thIs job and hIm beIng able to rIde wIth me don't get to comfortable wIth thIngs because thIngs always change out the blue that you wIll never expect so always suck up knowledge when you can. Because you never know when you'll be able to get this knowledge agaIn the way you got It the fIrst tIme. That really made me thInk when he saId that. As that sat In my mInd. I always re- member the certaIn thIngs he saId to me I was always a good lIstener. It was always certaIn thIngs that I wIll always remember when people speak. To me that regIsters In my mInd and wIll always be runnIng thru my mInd at tImes. After our lIttle talk we laid down and dOsed off tIred from drIvIng stIll pumped up and so, Happy I was workIng, but soon I feel asleep myself smIlIng from ear to ear just thInkIng how the day just went. Next day we got up early check the truck and the traIler tIres and for any leaks made sure all the lIghts were workIng opened the hood to checked the belts and make Sure they weren't to tIght our to lose everythIng was In good workIng condItIon. Then we headed down the road my pops was drIvIng then because he saId there were some hIlls ahead and that he'll take um untIl I get more mIles under my belt. We drove a couple hours then made It to New MexIco. The truck had Prepass and It gave us the green lIght as we entered each state so we passed the scale house to Inter New MexIco and rolled rIght on Into the TA truckstop. And O 'yea we were pullIng rIght Into that truck stop to get ready to go In freshen up and take a shower. Then we headed back down the road taken a shower wIth watching the clock we stIll wanted to stay In control of our tIme to cover good mIles for the day also. We TrIed to cover a certaIn amount of mIles a day so we can stay In good tImIng wIth the delIvery. EspecIally when they saId they wIll be a late fee so we wanted to make sure that we were there on tIme. We Had to make sure you be on tIme to your appoIntments out here. The broker the shipper and the receIver wIll fInd any kInd of way to make extra money. By chargIng me for thIs and chargIng me for that. I'm lIke what do you mean ? I mean any way someone can make some extra cash they wIll. You wanna be a truck drIver, You have to pay atten- tIon on all angles out here. I'm lIke ok It's all kInds of ways for people to get over If you don't know what's goIng on that's really wIld to me also. WhIle beIng out on the road my pops always saId you have to stop every three or four hours to stretch your legs to help wIth your blood cIrculatIon 'your sIttIng down all day so you wanna stop and stretch your legs every few hour. As we were rolling down the road tIme kInda was flyIng by we were gettIng hungry agaIn not knowIng to many places to stop at where you can pull In wIth your truck and traIler I knew we were gonna end back up at another truck stop to grab some truck stop specIal. As We ended up rollIng In to El Paso Tx and pullIng Into a Petro truck stop that I stopped at when I was wIth my frIend to hIt up the all you can eat buffet. Just thInkIng to myself how I made that decIsIon that I wanted to change what I was doIng and stayed commItted to my" decision "and took actIng on every step I needed to. It felt good to brIng myself back to a spot my frIend brought me too on my own, wIllIng to take actIon. I was makIng a decIsIon of my lIfe thIs was kInda of a specIal moment for me. wIth the Petro havIng the all you can eat, and as starvIng as we was wIth no doubt, that's what we were gonna order. As we went on In and washed our hands to head Into the food court I started talkIng to another guy there that was a truck drIver. As we got our food from the buffet we were stIll talkIng at that moment I let hIm know I was a new drIver and was new out here and was happy I found thIs truck stop. ThIs Is wana the fIrst places I stop at wIth a frIend my fIrst tIme on the road do to truckIng. I was just happy to be here. That's when he saId you should download the app to let you know you were the truck stops are and you can see What they have to offer before you get there so you don't have to waste tIme pulling off and on the freeway and they gIve you the exIt It's on. I'm lIke what are the names of these apps ?He says trucker tools and Dat and every truck stop should be lIsted on these apps to show you your optIons you have to choose from. I'm lIke cool started to download them whIle I was knockIng thIs food down. I Told hIm thanks as he was fInIshed up hIs food and was headed out. I downloaded the apps and fInIshed up eatIng hIt the restrooms then headed back to the truck to rest up and take our ten hour break before we headed back down the road. We rested up and took off the next day. So far my drIvIng was good It's been flatland so far and some small hIlls at the end of ArIzona but that was about It. My pops saId It's flat from here on out but It's some slIght more hIlls ahead but It's not that bad just drIve how you been and watch the rpms so you know when to shIt every load your gonna pull Is gonna be a dIfferent weIght so dependIng how heavy the loads are you wIll always know when to shIft by watchIng your rpms. So remover what I'm tellIng you because you never know how long you'll have someone wIth you to remInd you. I'm lIke I'm lIstenIng I hear you y you say that you bonIng out on me ?. He replIes. No just sayIng you really need to be payIng attentIon to how to operate and to remember and keep In mInd what I'm teachIng you out here. AgaIn I replIed I'm listening and I'm payIng attentIon I am. I know I'm thInkIng to myself he sure keeps sayIng that so that kinda stood out wIth me as, were rollin down the road, We stIll had a lot of mIles to knock out before the day was up so we coutenuId down the road but as the fuel was gettIng low. I called up the owner and let hIm know we needed more fuel so I had to call Angil agaIn for another com check so I called hIm to let hIm know we needed more fuel he saId he was gonna send It rIght over I'm lIke cool talk to you latter. As I was usIng the apps that the guy had me down load not only that they let you know where the gas statIon was they also told you the prIce of the dIesel they had at each of the statIons so I found a statIon In merIdIan ms called the space way whIch I notIced they had the cheapest fuel In our whole route and for mIles to come so I made sure we stopped there spe- cIally. It saId It had a dInner dIne In cafe whIch sounded real good spe- cIally couldn't wait to see what kInd of food they had at all thIs truck stops wIth my own eyes II really notIced that they aren't that many places to get some real food when on the road. I'm pretty sure they're out here you just have to know we're there are by me beIng new out here I don't know jack unless I looked somethIng up but not know If It was cool for a truck to pull up to It I dIdn't wanna take tIme to fInd out unless we had a lot of tIme to spear pops dIdn't really know any spots for thIs route eIther so we just kept our eyes open for somethIng convenIent beIng In the bIg truck I know I'm new out here but I'm thInkIng to myself why Isn't there that many food joInts by the freeway that would be convenIent for truckers because I dId notIce once I really started payIng attentIon to how many trucks be goIng up and down the hIghway whIch really was amazIng because I never really payed attentIon to how many trucks It takes to make the world go round., these were just thoughts runnIng thru my head whIle I was out on the road dIfferent sItuatIons and dIfferent thIngs hIghlIghted to me would always run threw my head lIke I had a small voIce talk to me as I was out on the road. But for some reason I thought It was someone tryIng to tell me somethIng but I dIdn't know or catch on to what It's tryIng to tell me. It would be just thIs crazy feeling I would get sayIng to myself well I guess thIs Is a piece of the puzzle In my lIfe that I have to fIgure out thIs Is somethIng I saId to myself that I had to fIgure thIs out or what thIs feelIng was I had. We were stIll headed down the road not to far from the drop around a few hundred mIles to go wIth all the drIvIng we were doIng. I was drIvIng stIll real scratchy wIth the gears but my pops dId not want to to get to tIred. But stIll wanted me to watch hIm. So I can pIck up more notes from hIm and how he drIves. WhIch I was taken as many notes as I could. I don't thInk he really knew how much I was thInkIng about gettIng Into thIs truckIng Industry I dIdn't know If he thought If I just wanted to drIve for myself or start off where I can to learn how to run the busIness based on how I could fIgure out, how to get started In the Industry perIod wIthout that much knowledge of runnIng an Independent company. But I ♥ knew I wanted to get my own company but I had a bIgger pItcher that. I couldn't explaIn at the tIme. I trIed to tell hIm how I was thInkIng but I don't thInk he could see or understand how I was tryIng to see thIngs. BeIng an entrepreneur I always remember that, we'll always have a vIsIon of thIngs In the world to where we'll see thIngs that's complex for people to fIgure out In a way where we see some- thIng dIfferent. DIdn't make It a bIg fuse just stayed alert. To everythIng that was goIng on and we traveled threw and made It to atlanta ga for our drop. As we made It to the drop there was a few truck In front of us so of course we had to get In lIne and check In when It's tIme. By us just pullIng In from off the road we both were ready to lay it down tell It was tIme to check back In to get unloaded. BeIng new I'm just layIng there restIng but was jumpIng up every 10 to 15 mIn to see what was goIng on wIth the process wIth thIs checkIng In so we can get unloaded. After a few hours of waItIng they called us to a door to get unloaded whIch took a few more hours at that tIme I asked my pops what's all the waIt. He says well If your gonna be haulIng produce your gonna be waItIng a lot at your pIckups and receIvers because they have to pulp certaIn products before loadIng them Into your traIler for pulp recorded trackers for certaIn load that re- quIre specIfIc attentIon when transported. ThIs how the produce haulIng goes you'll see you're just gettIng your ears wet. I'm startIng to see for myself and I knew from the start that thIs Is what I was goIng to be doIng. SInce I already told myself that thIs Is what I was goIng to be doIng I had to adjust. It wasn't so easy at fIrst but I told myself I would be tryIng my best at what I have to do to make the sItuatIon rIght. By thIs beIng a real lIfe changer for me. I knew It was gonna be a hell of an experIence for me but I loved every bIt of It. After we got unloaded I went Into the offIce to get the paperwork made shue It was all sIgned and the load was a clean delIvery. Headed back to the truck to call Angil to let hIm know we de- lIvered the load and got the paperwork and the load was a clean delIvery and what was I supposed to do now ? He says after you break or when you're ready we're gone pIck up a load In MIssIssIppI to take back to CalIfornIa. I'm lIke what part of MIssIssIppI he's says forest park MIssIssIppI Is where the load Is pIckIng up at. So we headed out to forest park after we got sItuated. After We headed out I had to call hIm back to ask hIm where dId he want us to go when we got to forest MIssIssIppI ? Are we pIckIng up soon as we get there.? He says he stIll waItIng on the load confIrmatIon for the load. Just go the the truck stop and waIt tell he calls me wIth the load InformatIon. There Is a truck stop down the hwy and there Is a restaurant there also. Stop there and get you somethIng to eat tell I get the load confIrmatIon to us so we get goIng I'm lIke ok. We headed out, Not to long after,

We got to thIs truck stop. That he had us go to and waIt It was out In the country wasn't to many places In thIs area so It wasn't that hard to fInd. We just drove a few hours from ATL to mIssIssIppI I was stIll a lIttle tIred so we rested up some more In the truck. We were hungry but we decided we was gonna go In after we rested for a about 20 mIn or so. WhIch we ended up fallIng asleep for about a hour or so. Then woke up to stIll see the Angel still hasn't called me back wIth the confirmatIon yet. Not really thInkIng about the tIme knowIng we been waItIng for up to 4 to 5 hours now. I was already thInkIng what my frIend told me when I was wIth hIm on that load that we had to do a 34 hour reset before we headed back to CalIfornIa as I was stIll adjustIng to how the flow of thIngs were goIng and for my pops keepIng me updated I would of been taken thIs waIt tIme a lIttle dIfferent. But agaIn beIng so happy to be drIven that It dIdn't bother me I just always have other thoughts that be runnIng threw my head as I'm always tryIng to fIgure somethIng out to see how I would handle It In my way. We ended up gettIng up and goIng Into the restraInt that was there and to get somethIng to eat beIng from CalIfornIa comIng out to mIssIssIppI. Never beIng here before seeIng how old the buIldIngs look then the places looked the same unless It was KFC or subway or a busIness that was In a bIg food chaIn a lot of busIness were In real old buIldIngs whIch Is kind of a weird look when comIng from CalIfornIa. We headed on Into go check In see what the food taste lIke. We sat down and check out the menu It dIdn't look too bad we order we the food came It had a lIttle dIfferent taste from beIng from CalIfornIa but the food, It was bomb let me tell you we knocked down all our food. BeIng As hungry as we were. It Wasn't that bad but nothIng to where we wanted to sIt there and keep eatIng It all day. But It dId do the job for the moment. We were so full we headed back to the truck to rest up some more. I never knew how all that drIven can have you beat up and tIred lIke that. We clImbed back up In the truck to get some more rest we both feel back to sleep I dIdn't even realIze how tIred I was tell I woke up a few hours later to fInd out that I stIll haven't got a call from Angel yet. By then I was well rested up now. To get back up to fInd myself gettIng hungry agaIn buy thIs tIme It's gettIng dark now not knowIng thIs town we dIdn't know where to go. We were on along hwy It wasn't really no traffIc so I decIded to drIve a bIt down the road to see If we saw another place to eat at. We headed down the road about a mIle and a half to see a bIg rIg parked at a small gas sta- tIon so I decIded to stop there to grab me some snacks. As I went InsIde I found out that they served hot food. The food was smIllIng so goodI had to go back to the truck to tell my pops to come In so he can see what he wanted because they dId have dIfferent optIons. I remembered I had order baked chIcken corn mash potatoes cabbage and my soda. I told my pops I'm glad I drove down the way whIch wasn't but about 2 mIles down the road. After we got our food we went back to where we were parked and contInue to waIt and eat our food we just got. The day was pretty much over wIth so we ate and was ready to go back to sleep. As I we was layIng down my pops says. I hope Angil calls In the am wIth the load conforma- tIon were well over our 34 hour break. I'm lIke man I know rIght. But I know Im call hIm In the mornIng If he doesn't call me by the tIme I get up to call hIm. Not upset just needIng to know what's goIng on and how long dId he thInk It was gonna take. I called hIm around 11 am MIssIssIppI tIme and he saId he was stIll waItIng for the broker who was gIvIng hIm the load InformatIon so he could send to us. Me thInkIng ok Is that what I'll be doIng In the future when I have someone workIng for me, that was a thought that ran threw my head those were the type of thoughts that ran threw my head whIle I was learnIng thIs whole process. So as we waIted for hIm to call back wIth me needIng to practIce and needIng more mIles I practIce goIng up and down thIs steep hIll to practIce tryIng not to scratch so much whIle we were empty as we waIted for hIm to call back wIth the load confIrmatIon. I thought this would be the best thIng for me to do especIally the way thIngs was fallIng together I need to take advan- tage of every chance I get If Its gonna better myself lIke my pops saId you better get It all whIle you can cuz If mIght not come your way the same way. It dId now whIle my pops sat back and watched the way thIng were flowIng. And saId you sure pIck up on thIngs pretty quIck. As we waIted for the call I drove up and down the highway goIng back and forth over thIs hIll for a whIle. As I drove back to the truck stop to park. Not notIcIng as I was drIvIng I would be holden the steerIng wheel so tIght that now I'm startIng to feel all the paIn in My for arms from constantly holdIng the steerIng wheel so tIght. I'm lIke pops thIs drIvIng can have you really tIred and my four arms are kInd of sour. He replIes yes that's why you have to get your rest when you're out here on the road and that's another reason why they say you have to do a 34 hour reset after drIvIng so many hours In a workweek especIally when you're drIvIng a cross country and thats why Its a 70 hour work week to lImIt the hours you drIve to you keep you safe when you are out on the road to gIve you the abIlIty to regroup wIth yourself so you can operate safely when you're out on the road. And that's one of the reasons why the hIghway patrol ask to see your logbook to make sure you're obeyIng all the laws rules and regulations of the log book So pay attentIon or you wIll get a tIcket and be workIng for the man wIth no choIce so I'll be helpIng you wIth It as long as I'm wIth you so I can teach you as much as I can so sucknall thIs InformatIon up Im gIvIng you. At that tIme I dIdn't even know how to do the log book but I got the job wIth my master traIner thIs Is just my learnIng process. Because In the truckIng school I attended then dIdn't cover logbooks. So at fIrst he would walk me through everything as I picked up on it he'll just do the log book for me tIll I fIgured the basIcs of what I needed to do so I wouldn't get a tIcket when the hIghway patrol ask to see the log book because they wIll be pullIng you over you just don't never know when. But when they do you wanna have all your paperwork In order nIce and neat and you shouldn't have any problems even tho there always tryIng to fInd somethIng wrong or try and sIght you for somethIng so you wanna make sure you have all your stuff In order that you need. Every tIme he would do the log books he would explaIn everythIng he was doIng, having to go over it multiple times but not gettIng It all at once but I was learnIng lIttle at a tIme whIle, I had to suc up all the thIs InformatIon from all angles of what I needed to learn whIle In the drIver seat. The logbook Is consIstent wIth all actIon that you take In the truck whIle on the clock. He told me every tIme you start your day It's lIke checkIng In to work and keepIng track of your hours. ThIs meant every tIme you stopped you where to show stop tIme how long you were there and where you end up at at every poInt of the day your movIng around also keepIng track of the mIles that you travel through all the states and a lot of thIs InformatIon has to be turned In In order to get paId for my work week No a days they have EID elections logging devices that will keep track of all the for you. The mIles that we had to keep track of was for," Ifta" thIs Is a fuel tax you have to pay on for all the gallons you purchase, In every state. Every state has Its dIfferent sale tax to add up. To the gallons you purchased also have to mentIon what state you purchased the fuel In. Yes thIs Is called road tax. Another hIghlIght to me about what you have to keep a record of as beIng your own boss going fully independent. Always thInkIng to myself how fast tIme flIes and thIs tIme next year as long as I stay actIve and follow thru what I need to take care of for my busIness. I wIll be In another posItIon wIth more knowledge as long as I stay focused. I knew when I needed to get In the posItIon to get and make thIngs happen for me when the tIme came for me to get my own truck and start taken the steps I needed. As I was sIttIng there I was goIng over the logbook tryIng to understand It more. GoIng over the ones we dId sInce we drove all the way from CalIfornIa I was stIll tryIng to understand the work hour schedule to on duty and off duty safety checks mIles of trIp and addIng them up so at the bottom of each work day you had a 24 hour work day wIth proper brakes this is how it is done using Paper logs. BeIng new I'm tryIng my best to suck It all up. We ended up stayIng there another nIght. In the mornIng the boss called and says he has the load InformatIon. He was gonna send It over. It took about ten mIns when I got It we headed over to the PIck up address. I put the address In the gps and headed there to see for myself how thIs process Is goIng on. As we arrIved we had to turn down a dIrt road that was kInd of long as we pulled up to the address It's was a lIve chIcken ranch. So I kInda see what all the waIt was about specIally I know how It went last tIme. When I was just rIdIng wIth my frIend. SInce I had been to a chIcken ranch before I kInda knew what to expect especIally my pops already saId, Get use to waItIng because If you don't you can let the pace of thIngs piss you off so just take your tIme even. If It takes a lIttle longer than you thInk. We knew we were In for the waIt so we found a parkIng spot. Then found my way to the shIppIng and receIvIng offIce to check In and see how long the waIt was they let me know that there were seven trucks In front of me so o yea we had some more rest tIme before we got ready to head back down the road. I had to leave my phone number wIth them In the offIce and they saId to check the traIler temp make sure it's set and we'll call you when It's tIme to back

Into a door. Headed back to the truck to park and waIt were they wanted to and waIt for the phone call. Pops saId we'll be here tIll In the mornIng I dIdn't put It past hIm so we just layed on down In the truck to rest up tIll they called It wasn't nothIng to do or no we're to go whIle waItIng so at thIs tIme glad we had snakes In the truck because we sure wasn't able to get to anythIng to eat or drInk. As we laid there and fell asleep It wasn't tIll the 3 am that we had got the call to back Into a door to start gettIng loaded we backed In and waIted tell they fInIshed. It was stIll early In the am so we fell back to sleep. By the tIme they were done loadIng us up we had dId our safety check and had got the logbook ready to head out once they fInIshed. Once I headed back Into the offIce to receIve the paperwork for the load then I called Angel to let hIm know we were loaded up and that we needed the fuel advance for the rIde back. I gave hIm a call and he saId gIve hIm a few mIns and he'll call me back In a few mInutes I'm lIke ok. Az we waIted we headed on down to the truck stop to waIt tell he sent It over. So I looked up the closest bIg truck stop because It was definitely Time for a shower wIth sIttIng up them days In the truck just waItIng. I end up fIndIng the closest truck stop was a love's truck stop so we made our way over there to fInd out they do the same thIng that the TA does when you purchase 50 gallons and more In dIesel they wIll gIve you a free shower and add poInts to your card to where you can purchase thIngs from them when they add up. As we waIted for the fuel advance we got our stuff ready to hIt the showers. The boss had sent over the advance so we fueled up then headed over to park so we could shower and freshen up so we can start our day. FeelIng fresh and on top of that we got to get an earlIer start. we came out feelIng brand new we ended up gettIng somethIng to eat from arby's and a few snakes out the store headed back to the truck to head down the road. Pops started off drIvIng but eventually we swItched. As We drove back I started to pay attentIon to the small hIlls and the bIgger ones. I never really payed atten- tIon to the road the way I look at It In the truck. WhIle In a car you never even really know when It started to go up and down hIlls and around mountaIns on the road. When drIvIng the truck makes you really look at the road In a dIfferent vIew. There weren't that many hIlls comIng back threw LouIsIana and on Into texas It was pretty much a smooth rIde. We covered some good mIles that day startIng of early and headIng straIght down the road and freshenIng up. WhIch Is cool when you get to start your day earlIer In the mornIng somethIng about a fresh start that gets you goIng. We made It to the truck stop and got some rest after we ran our hours for the day. WhIch was good so It was gonna keep us In good tImIng for the drop we have to make, so you wanna make sure you keep up wIth the tIme whIle you're changIng the dIfferent tIme zones. You have to make sure your tImIng Is gonna have you On tIme for your delIvery. We rested up and fueled up freshened up and headed on back down the road to CalIfornIa. We dIdn't make It to our drop tIll the next day and was stIll a lIttle early for the drop. After checkIng In they went ahead and gave us a door so we can start gettIng unloaded. They dIdn't even take that long to unload us whIch Is crazy after all we been doIng Is been havIng to waIt at the pick ups Now no wait at the drop. Pops says see when you're ready to waIt and there's no waIt that's makes you feel good so don't get mad or upset wIth anyone, when you do 'It could have you waItIng longer you just gotta get use to the way thIngs kInda go out here I'll say in truck- Ing. After droppIng the load we headed back to the yard to park the truck and to pIck up my payment as he saId I'll get paId once I get back to the yard. WIth all the paperwork for my payment processIng. As we pulled Into the yard wIth the truck so we pulled Into and parked and started gettIng our stuff out of the truck and puttIng It In my car. Then went Into the offIce were Angel was. He was on the phone when I walked In, after he hang up then he asked. How did I lIke the trIp I saId well I can't com- plaIn work as usual then he ask when wIll I be ready to head back out. I replIed gIve me a few days and we'll be ready to head back out. He Says Just was tryIng to see If we were on the same page I have my guy here pIckIng the truck up after It gets servIced he's going to pIck up his load and head out. But when he gets back just wanted to make sure that you'll be ready to head out. SInce your fresh back on the road just wanted to make sure you get your rest to be ready to roll out tell you get back In the swIng of thIngs. That's when I meet, Block he was a older guy probably in his forties. He's been workIng for thIs guy looks like so I guess he was just tryIng to keep thIngs movIng to make thIngs add up for what he was doIng Is all I can thInk about how he kept thIs truck movIng but when lookIng at the pItcher when not beIng the drIver why would you want the truck to stop if you can keep It rollIng. NIce busIness Is what I was thInk- Ing but I know I had a whole lot of work to do to get Into that posItIon. But I was all In for It thIs was a good hIghlIght for me. I really payed at- tentIon to what he had all goIng on at the yard' on how he was makeIng an Income. WhIle he was In busIness having the trucks run up and down the Highway whIch let me know he had more than one way goIng on to make an Income. WhIch I thought was great, I love multIply types of Income especIally to see how you can put somethIng together from hands on experIence'. Then to see hIm hungry for more I'm mean to make more money I dIdn't know If that was good for hIm or bad. I just know thIngs had to work for you If you knew how to manages It, That's a thought that would always run threw my head. We dIdn't have any problems whIle we were out on that trIp so I know he made a nIce pIece of change also so I was really concerned just thInkIng to myself If that was a sIgn of a stress or what but It seemed lIke somethIng 'was up. I just couldn't poInt It out at the tIme. But I paId attentIon to as much as I can when I came around to what was goIng on to try and pIck up any Info or anythIng that I thought. I needed to Put In my box of my Ideas I knew one day that I would understand that feelIng he was goIng through especIally. If I was gonna own my own truckIng company one day one day. I would be In that posItIon or could be close to understandIng what he was goIng threw at that tIme. As I just went wIth the flow the way thIngs was goIng. I couldn't complaIn because not too many people that I knew or came across got rollen In the way I dId wIth my pops. That can explaIn to me any method to get rollen. My pops even kept sayIng thIs, Put that whole ex- pressIon that Angel had remInded me when I was on the way out on that run wIth my frIend. When he had Ac problems on the way to atlanta but the expressIon he gave and how I took It was I guess it was the level of problems they were havIng. But I stIll saId to myself I was In It for the rIde. Just dIdn't know If It was worth It or not. But at the tIme who could I ask I dIdn't have any Idea who to ask at the tIme. That's what was goIng thru my mInd. He pulled hIs checkbook out and wrote me a check for $1500.00. I was so excIted I had made my fIrst check. Just thInkIng I stuck to my Ideas went to work got paId when I got back and had enjoyed the tIme wIth my pops on the road because the tIme me and my pops spend together has been rare. We haven't really spent that much tIme to- gether It wasn't tIll I was a teen ager when I started to see my pops so It was a lot of tIme spent not hangIng around each other. It wasn't tIll I was around 13 years old when I remember my pops pullIng up In a bIg black KW. Kenwwod for short truck. I would never forget that day never thInk- Ing that I would be drIvIng a bIg rIg when I got older but my father was In and out of my lIfe. All I know I would see hIm every once In awhIle It wasn't when he came back from hIs trIp. He was just gone I never knowIng what had goIng on. I just knew It would be long perIods of tIme between me seeIng hIm agaIn. BeIng a kId not understandIng a lot of thIngs but rememberIng a lot. As I got older we started to hang out a lIttle more than before but stIll not that much. All I knew was when he dId come around we would just enjoy the tIme that we would spend together even If It was just gettIng somethIng to get or just puttIng somethIng on the grIll. As I was a kId when he would dIsappear and I dIdn't see hIm It was lIke when I was In the car wIth who ever I was wIth, when I saw a bIg black truck I would always look to try and see who was In the drIver seat never saId nothIn to nobody about that that. That's just what I dId nobody never knew tIll I wrote It In thIs book but hey I'm In It for the long haul rIght. NothIng wrong wIth always wonderIng where he was but I never let that feelIng stop me from doIng and thInkIng what I wanted to do. I know that why he had to express and make me understand hIs ways whIch I dId but he really dIdn't know me how I husle or how I really put stuff together and make stuff happen so I just remaIned the student for the time tIll It was tIme for me to take actIon, on how I do thIngs then he wIll see for hImself how I really do thIngs when I put my mInd to It. But he was goIng to see when that tIme wIll soon come. After I Got The check me and my pops went to the bank. The bank was rIght down the street to cash the check. Me and my pops dId not talk about any pay so me when I came out the bank I asked pops what he needed for comIng out and helpIng me out on the road. He saId he'll take $500.00 If I'm cool wIth that I saId well I couldn't of made any of thIs money wIthout your, "help" at least the way thIngs got goIng for me out here out the blue. So I gave hIm the $500.00. Pops Is cool Im cool Im lIke It's good he's smIllIng I'm smIllng. I gave pops a huge and saId I made It happen, "he was lIke you're sure dId I gotta gIve It to you you got too much jelly for the donut. Crazy How I went lookIng for somethIng didn't know how things will happen. It really seemed lIke everythIng has been fallIng rIght together In a way that I was tryIng to make happen Is really is ImpressIve. My pops starts to tell me what he use to tell my mother when I was In her stomach you were gonna be real specIal we always talked and prayed on her belly all the tIme when she was pregnant wIth me that's why He says he gave me my name Khafra also reads Khafre whIch was the son of KIng Khufu, Khafra buIlt the second largest pyramId In GIza In 2500 BC hIs name also meanIng Master TraIner, Master buIlder. Pops says he new I would lIve up to the name the he gave me whIle he prayed over me whIle I was In her stomach. We were both happy about the trIp and that we could spend the tIme together and teach me somethIng that wIll help me be successful out here on the road. So I let pops know that he saId that Block Is headed out and when he gets back he'll be ready for us to roll out agaIn If we're up to It. He Says Yea. I can't leave you yet you stIll have some learnIng to do I'm lIke cool I'll let you know when Angel calls I'll give you a heads up to get ready to roll back out he says ok I'm goIng to go wash up and get some rest just let hIm know and then we went on our way. He stayed In downtown los angeles and I stayed In compton whIch Is about 35 mIn from each other. Just really so surprIsed wIth myself what I really just dId and then come back home wIth the money In my pocket and payed pops. Just made me feel so good. But I even felt better because I was able to support my famIly In a way. That Just made me feel so good jumpIng straIght In to trying and fIgure the steps to jumpstart a cartIer In the truckIng Industry when everyone says It's gonna be awhIle before you wana get your own truck and company I never understood the people that saId that. I never let that bother me In my of maken of thIngs. When I seen that you could make a stable Income when your stayIng busy and knowIng how to keep your trucks movIng. BeIng A drIver dependIng on how much money you're tryIng to make a month depends on the posItIon you have to decide you want when In busIness. For me I Was just gettIng started and I didn't know why or for what but I did know I wanted to know how to run a business so I had to stIck around the truckIng Industry a whIle. To get the knowledge I needed to Get me goIng. Always thInkIng about how much money I'll be makIng once I got the whole Independent part down. KnowIng just havIng thIs amount of Income wasn't what I was lookIng for but I had to start somewhere to get started and seeIng how thIng was flowIng and talkIng just to a few folks on the road how they got started I knew I had to take advantage wIth thIngs, when I could wIth all thIs truckIng stuff. Im mean GettIng started In all to see how I wanted to operate and get thIngs goIng for me. I was really tryIng to see what posI- tIon I was goIng to target whIle In these Industry just tryIng to see the the bigger pItcher ahead. For myself to gIve me an update decIsIon on what I wanted to do. After doIng some research tryIng to fInd InformatIon about How to start a busIness and what levels to reach were I had to fInd InformatIon as I looked it was lIke someone really has to walk your through the steps that's been threw them I mean you can find the laws and rules and regulations but when it comes to hands on on a one on one like a coach it was just these huge trucking companies that will train you in a way to just work for them other then that you'll fInd yourself searchIng and searchIng for InformatIon. As I made It to the house my famIly was so happy for me that I made a decIsIon to do somethIng out the blue to make a change I SaId I was goIng to do It and made It come Into exIstence to show them I could and prove to them you can do what you want out here it was a good feelIng for everybody my family I mean especIally the way the struggle Is set up Its real In the fIeld. To make a decent Income Is a blessIng and I know It gets greater later so we had to celebreIght for a new begInnIng whIch wIll open the doors for even more beautIful Ideas. We all got ready to roll out and enjoy the evenIng. Another busIness where you heard you can be real successful In fInancIally. And you get to travel and see all parts of the US dependIng on where you wanna dive to. By me reachIng a lot of dIfferent companIes and askIng questIon. From other drIvers who drove and are stIll drIvIng for there companIes wIll send you to all 48 states especIally If you're In traInIng they gonna keep you out for 45 days and you wIll be drIvIng full shIfts thIs Is to get as many mIles under your belt to help you understand and getting your body fit and get the knowledge you suppose have to operate the truck because It doesn't matter how fast of a learner you are there is no rushIng thIs process It really takes time and hands on training to learn the process to see both ends the driver side and the broker side, but when you get It you got It. WIth the dIfferent restrIctIons that are dIfferent wIth each company and each com- pany had there own way they operated. ThIs Is what I had to decide from when tryIng to make a decIsIon on whIch choice the will push me to go Independent also. As I enjoyed my tIme off and was happy I can celebrate for an experIence lIke thIs and I was glad I could hIghlIght the actIon to my kIds as they watch me take thIngs to the next level just happy I can show them the blueprInt, "to get to the next level as long as you commIt to something and put tIme In and effort you wIll gaIn progress and suc- cess. I told them don't never be scared to take a rought as long as you know you're doIng rIght never block a vIsIon you see you wIll never know the outcome tIll you try it. As I talked to my gIrl I told her I can't waIt to learn to operate thIs truck alone i'm going to work for a while till i'm able to get my own truck. Since i know i'll be doing this for a while. She was really happy for me especially because a lot of people that we grew up with and went to school with wasn't doing nothing positive with there life. our err of growing up most of our err of folks we grew up with the most successful ones that had jobs worked at the refinery. I thought about it for a while growing up in high school because that's when it hit the high school while everyone was thinking what they could do to make a large amount of income. Or a good income being independent at a young age. As i got older i focused what and how to find someway to make a great income were you didn't have to struggle if you could get in and pass the test. But just like everything else that when it's put in front our you inhofe that it will get your attention. So I was really happy that i found something that made good money that fit the process. As we waited for that Phone call from Angel. To Go back down the road. It wasn't till the next day he called and asked if I would be ready the head out tomorrow picking up the in salinas ca to go to Atlanta ga. Im like yup cool see you tomorrow so I hit my pops up to let him know that I got the call and he ask if I will be ready to head out tomorrow so I told him I would be so will you be ready to roll out. He says yea man what time. He said tomorrow evening so we can start picking up the next day. That's a nice drive to start in the evening. Cool I'll call you in the morning to see what time you'll be ready then we'll roll up there to the yard. The yard was about 35 min away from both of us before we would get there from our distance depending on the traffic. In the morning around that time I called the Angel to see what time he needed us to come down there. He said to come around 2 o'clock I said ok and hung up and called to let my pops to let him know. That Angel what's us to be at the yard by 2 pm. He said ok I'll meet you up there. As I hang up so excited that we're getting ready to roll back out on another trip with my pops. Not because Pops's teaching me but we get to spend more time together to get to know Each other a little more than we did. Thinking to myself it's crazy all of a sudden out of all the times when my pops is not around. But my pops popped up around in a time of my life when I really needed some help to better myself as an entrepreneur with a rought that he really could help me with. Sometime family will not support you or motivate you when they can't see what you see but when one is there to support you in a way a it's the real meaning of support no looking for nothing in return really means something. Thinking to myself maybe this is meant for me. My pops always tells me when allah has a message to deliver he puts his soldiers to work if don't complete the task you won't be crowned to your kingdom. I always tried to understand pops when he would speak on certain things and I would try my best to understand the call to the messenger so maybe we're upposed to be a trucker those are the thoughts that are running threw my head. But the more I think about it to myself, I say to myself. As I think about trucking, I think about owning running my own company. I didn't want to be just a trucker but I was going to take every step I seen that would help me learn about running my own company. I always told myself one step is always one step closer to success but to know how many steps to take will determine on how productive you are. As I got myself ready to roll out. I had packed up already just was going over my things that make sure that I had everything I needed, you know you can be so excited about going somewhere that you might forget something so I just wanted to make sure that I didn't forget anything because it's a lot going up and down on the road and by have to keep taken all your stuff in and out of the truck when getting back to the yard i needed to make sure. I Have all my gadgets you needed but of course it was always something else that you needed or want As it got closer to the time to leave to the lot i wanted To leave early so I can be a hour early. Because i did know how traffic was gonna be to get therein good timing I wanted to make sure that i had everything i needed. As I Got there I checked in with Angel to get all the information i needed on the load conformation while I was driving to get the load information for the load we had to pick up. Then I walked back to the truck to get my stuff to put in the truck. While I was putting my stuff in the truck that's when my pops was pulling into the yard. With a big smile on his face saying are you ready to roll out champ. As he parks and starts to load up his stuff into the truck grabbing a few items and as we're loading up my pops says he brought his CB this time since it wasn't one in the truck so he says he'll hook it up once we stopped after we got rollen we got a nice drive to up to northern ca from we're the yard was it was about a 6 ½ or 7 hour drive up north from where we were. I started off driving but I knew we would have to switch soon because. I still had problems climbing the steep incline when it came to the downshifting I still had to practice more and needed more time to get the hang of it. As we got closer to the grape vine we switch seats and llet him drive up to the first drop. I just need more miles under my belt. That's what I told myself I thought that i would be able to learn the shifting process as fast as i learned how to drive a car stick shift but i was wrong it was no rushing this process in learning this, this was gonna take a little longer to learn this process. At this time i am telling myself that i do need more time to prac- tice when it's coming to learning this process while I can because ain't no telling how long this is going to last working with this guy and being able to have my pops riding with me to help train me in the process of how things are going. So on this trip i was going to really focus on reading the rpms so i could know when to shift the gears when first starting of watch- ing the rpms. Just being new trying to pay attention to all the things you have to operate the truck can be real confusing when getting started and trying to stay in full control of the and down shifting seems to be a bit confusing tell you get the hang of things. We had more than one pick up so we headed to sillines California then to Delano California to pick up both of the picks. They loaded us up pretty fast. I got the see for myself that the wait thing is only sometimes that what I Got to see how, quick we got loaded at both of the places we're we picked up at I told myself I'll just have to go with the flow of things. After getting loaded up we headed back down to head over the grape vine to jump on i5 as I was rolen by the time I got to the 225 mark you can fill like the truck doesn't wanna go any faster you can actually fill the wait that you're pulling in the trailer. With my foot to the floor to get a full acceleration and power to climbing the hill. The and higher we got up the grad I had to shift properly so the truck can keep moving. the higher you got the slower the truck started to go, the more you had to downshift in order to keep the truck moving. As I started to down shit again being a little nervous and being a little rusty and with all the cars and the trucks being so close on my tail I became nervous and missed the gear and brought the truck to a complete stop. But remember- ing what my pops saying. Make sure that your hazards are on stop and start over just him telling me these simple steps made it easier for me to click into safety mode quick and get back moving. That was another saying that just stuck in my head that I knew that would stay with me. So yes I made sure the hazard were on got the truck to the side of the road got the truck back into first gear and started climbing back up the hill. Watching the Traffic s the truck started pulling up the hill my pops sees what I'm doing, still worried about the traffic behind me to where he seen me trying to rush he says another key safety tip stop worrying about the traffic behind you that's making you think you have to rush, when not knowing what to do you will tear the truck gears if you do not operating properly so take your time and watch your Rpms and switch when it's time. Those simple words again helped me so much in a time you felt like you had to make a quick decision and staying com at the same time so I climbed the hill slowly paying attention. I've gotten the truck to its climbing gear. Yes I was still a little nervous but I wasn't giving up with that being said. I climbed the the hill for my first time with a loaded trailer I was so happy for myself yes I Will be ready next time but I know I needed more hill climbing ex- perience to do and I was looking forward to it.

There wasn't a any more hill climbing going down I 10 on the way till we hit chowchilla ca and going through Arizona on I 10 and going into Tucson Az was a little hill climbing. We stopped at the Triple T truck stop to break and grab something to eat not to many places on the high- way had restraints to get something to eat from beside Taco

Bell, Mcdonald's, Arby's which was the only other spot to eat for a while. Triple T was the spot to stop at if you wanted to get you something to eat cooked in a kitchen. Plus there is a Stoe In the back of the parking lot just in case you didn't wanna go into the truck stop to eat or felt like walking thru there huge parking lot so this is a cool exit to stop at when running across Arizona, we rested up and I noticed that the next hill climbing was after we left the Triple T as we got to New Mexico it was pretty much smooth sailing we would stop every three or four hours of driving every time we were driving so that we could stretch our legs and walk around so we could keep blood circulation in our legs that's a real huge health problem out here. When sitting for long periods of time It's unhealthy and bad on you. You need to get up when you can to help with the circulation to stay healthy. You want to practice certain things. To keep yourself healthy while on the road. My pops would highlight things to keep me aware so i can stay on top of things when operating the truck to staying healthy and staying in a healthy condition while on the road. Which is a good thing because everyone that has a cdl or got close to getting one know you have to take a physical and be enrolled into a physical program in order to hold a valid cdl they use to give out green medical cards when i started out. Now they updated your information into the computer so when the highway patrol pulls you over they can see your status in the system to let them know you're up to date with your physical. Which meant you were valid to operate a commercial vehicle on the highway. Not being updated with your physical can have you put out of service. Nobody wants to be put out of services believe me. These things are good to know And also make part of your daily task if your gonna be out on the road and be driving long distance in a truck or a car this is a good health tip to know. As we continued down the road going threw texas we took i20. I 20 was pretty smooth not too many hills pretty much a straight a way being from California and the speed limit being 55 then Arizona's bring 75 mph but Texas being 80 mph I was like dang we really can go 80 mph out here i'm like like wow. But as i looked around there was nothing for miles and miles and miles away so i said i guess that's why and probably being the biggest state of all that may be the reason but i don't really know it was just a suprising to me how the speed limit is 80 mph. I wasn't going to go 80 mph but that sure did catch my attention we still were headed down the road of course we needed more fuel by know so i called Angel to let him know so he can send over the express code so we can fuel back up. So he says he's gonna send it over in a minute i'm like cool while waiting for the express code i started to look up to see where we would fuel up at so we'll receive our free shower points so we didn't have to pay for one because i did notice that we don't get reim- bursed for them when getting paid for the money we spent on showers. Paying for showers on the road can get pretty expensive if you don't pay attention and saving money any chance you get on the road is a blessing. I tried to take advantage of them when there wasn't a cheap fuel stop that would bet there price and make me wait till the next big truck stop to shower. Because the way the shower are set up at the main truck stops you'll be trying your best to make it there to shower because how nice and clean they are Just A truck stop tip I picked up on the road while i was working for Angel he never really said anything about any thing with the truck or what was going on he never asked how we was doing or any- thing. While gone on the road. I noticed every time i would call him to ask for the fuel because it wasn't really no other reason to call it would just be a quick convo. I was just thinking to myself by not knowing me or my pops to let someone go down the road and don't check on them but was so worried about if the load was good and delivered in good condition with clean bills. With this being my third load with this guy i noticed that he would always be tynced up with a slit attuid never really happy i don't know this guy but that's the feeling i got every time i talked to him. That is what i was thinking to myself. When i was doing construction and i had to put together a work crew and put them to work i would check on them and made sure things were going smoothly but not to check on them at all, that was not in the books so yes this did catch my attention while i was in this man's truck working for him. That didn't fit right with me and that's why my pops kept saying suck all this up you don't know how long this will last. These was the thoughts that was ruling threw his mind as well with my mind being a business owner with workers. I don't know why i always thought of business strategies when i thought of things. By me not knowing the whole outlook on how things went i just payed very close attention to what my pops had to teach me and tips im picking up from other drivers. Angel never gave any tips to how to prepare yourself for the road, how to save money, make a budget or even highlight on how to learn how to save your money in case you can't make it to work for a while or anything No kinda business tips at all. He was just so worried if we delivered the load and had clean bills so he can get paid for each load which i thought was strange. I would want both of us to know how to make ends meet at least when you know someone is new to the oper- ations. This is just something i did and thought about when i'm running my business. I would always kept a lot of the ways he handled his drivers in my head just to keep me informed on how to treat a driver when in my position while trying to take things to the next level in the trucking in- dustry. The next truck stop was a loves truck stop so i decided to stop there to fuel up so we can get our shower points added to our card we ended up pulling up to the pump right when the boss sent over the com chk with the fuel advance so we can fuel up. So we went inside to use the restroom and to pay for the fuel i noticed every time we stopped at the loves. They were extra clean i liked that. I hated to stop at a truck stop to find out that there restroom is very nasty. Some don't care about a clean restroom and how that can slow your business down owning a truck stop specifically if this is your rough and you know the restroom is nasty you're gonna make sure to see if you can make it to a clean one even if you don't have to use it there, missing business as a business owner is important to notice at least that's my opinion. I know i'm passing up a nasty truck stop every time if I know that's there Get down being nasty But loves is one of the truck stops that hits the list for a stop pulse there everywhere once you start paying attention. Always driving a car i had never heard of a loves ♥ Stop being from California in the los angeles there are no major truck stops like that in the Los Angeles area there mostly are when you leave that part of Cali I didn't notice that until i started traveling more when i got older. We fueled up the truck and the trailer. The trailer has a separate gas tank then from the truck the truck has two 100 gallons tanks and the trailer has a 50 gallon fuel tank. we fuel up then headed back down the road we knew we were gonna make it half way threw texas but we knew we were gonna stop somewhere to stretch our legs between time. If you know texas you better have you some snacks and some more stuff driving thru there especially because itt seems like forever just to driving through texas. We ended up taken our next break at another. Loves truck stop so we could shower up and be ready for the next day. we didn't want to kill to many hours on on duty. So we tried to keep up with the miles so we could stay ahead of the clock this can help you to cover good miles for the day and good time ig if things went smooth. As we started the next day we did our safety check then use the restroom got some coffee then headed back to the truck so we can go An head down the road then i started to noticed we we're getting closer to we're me and my friend JoJo had stopped and got some BBQ. I had to make sure that we stopped there to get something to get. And I know the food was good Soulman's BBQ in royse city Tx. When we say this is the spot to stop when you're hungry and passing thru Texas yes ex 540 on i20 is the spot and I will try every- time I pass this way to stop and grab a bite We drove a couple more hours before we got there as we exited the highway you can smell it as we did pulled in and my pops smelled it even more as we was pulling up he was like O 'yea. Man this smells bomb, we needed this in our life" right now. Is hungry as you can get on the road with this going on oh yea there winning yes sir you know we have to take something to go for latter. We both ordered the same thing when we ordered Baked chicken, cabbage baked beans potato salad and a roast beef sandwich and a order to go, when I get done. We sat there and got so full. I didn't wanna move for a min" man this was bomb "After that we tighten up and got ready to head back down the road again, it wasn't but a few more hours before we got to Louisa. As we drove thru there I noticed there were no hills really going down I20 was pretty much a flat straight away. We took a short break then kept on rollin into Mississippi driving thru these states seemed like it didn't take no time at all to drive threw this states we ended up stopping In meridian Mississippi at the spaceway truck stop I noticed that there fuel was really cheap as I looked on the app I noticed yea it was the cheap- est fuel stop for miles out they also had the free shower when you fueled over 50 gallons. We were low on fuel so I called Angel so he can send over a fuel advance as we stopped there. We decided To fuel up and take our break there they had a dinner area there also As we took our break I de- cided to give my fried Antonio a call this was my friend that got me this job and let him know how all this was going and we had stopped at this spaceway truck stop, He asked if we had ordered yet and i'm like not yet we about to order he said to Order the fish sandwich and order the fries with gravy. I'm like ok I'm going to order just that. I'll let you know what it do, I'm about to order it when I'm done, Now let me see whatcha talking about. Then he says sounds like you're out there makin it do what it do just hang in there. I'm like yes you know I I got this I know need to learn a lot more but I'm in motion I know. I need more miles under my belt but I'm good pops making sure I'm operating this bad boy right Man I'm so happy you got me this job Big Dog. Man he said man you know I have to look out for my dog I grew up with man it's hard out here if we can help each other Im all in. Man for real I really appreciate it man you just don't know the feeling I have about this, thank you he says fasho dog just make sure you can learn all you can learn and don't fuck nothing up and pay attention to your reefer to make sure you don't get any claim on any loads cause you won't get paid. I'm like wow but that's the rules. And I'm going to see if he can get you some more cash since you got your pops in the truck with you. I'll let you know I have to call him anyways I'm like cool hell yea. He says yea I know he's going thru a lot of problems with his wife but I'll still let him know because you guys can keep that truck moving. I'm like cool but you know what. I kinda figured he had some- thing going on it sounded like that every time I talked to him I noticed he wasn't in so much of a good mood and I don't even know him. Yea man don't let that bother you just stay focused and alert man because you can easily get distracted from the road when you get up set behind the wheel if you can't control it. Not saying you can't I just wanted to but this in your head while on the road when you get upset behind the wheel can cause a big distractions so just keep this thought I use when Im trying to stay as com as possible when driving this big truck out here on the road cause anything can happen n a blink of an eye. Ok I got you thanks for the tips and I'll keep you posted on how things work out Man if your girl calls you and pis you of just tell her you'll call her back. I know man this can cause a big distraction so always stay alert and just let them know you'll call them back you'll thank me later n the long run fasho I got you and that will be the first thing I think of if that's a comes to be. After we hung up I sure went to order that fish sandwich and the fries with gravy to see what it do and what my friend was bragging about. My pops ended up ordering the same thing. The pieces I had of fish was so big and the gravy was dark, with crispy fries we dug in to figure out it was just what he was talking about. this joint was bomb the fish was crispy but still juicy and the fries was so bomb I haven't had the fries with gravy. but I tell you it was a nice hook up. I had to call him back to let him know o yea man that joint was fire I haven't had that twist before but I tell you they got it. I'm ordering gravy from n my fries whenever I can. He was like told ya man I'll keep you posted on what goes on out here and let you know how I'm hanging in there. After we ate we did our reset. Then got up did our safety check and fixed our log book then headed down the road. I'm still rusty with the log I didn't really learn the log book that fast it was taken me a little time while I tried to catch on to really understanding it. But trying to learn everything at one time was kind of a lot for me but I wanted to learn it so bad that I just went with the flow of how things was going. Because the main thing. I Was doing was making money So I just really went with the flow trying to learn as much as I could but we tightened up and headed down the road. We weren't to for out from Atlanta once we left the truck stop we made it to the drop and the wait process wasn't that bad he got the bills signed and headed back to the truck and then called the boss to let him know we dropped the load and everything came off clean Mr what are we supposed to do. He said to head back to the same truck stop in Mississippi that we were at last time rest up and get something to eat and he'll let us know with the load info. Since we knew we had some time to waste so we headed to the truck stop that was close by to take a break before we headed back down the road. We took a break there grabbed us some goodies then headed out to Mississippi. We made it to the truck stop after dark. We were still a little tired from the ride. So we just really parked and then went to sleep which before we head back towards California we had to do a 34 hour reset before headed back in that direction. Your rest is really important while out here in the road because if you don't know your stopping point when you know you need to too shut it down you can drive yourself off the road and kill yourself or even kill other people and nobody wants to even experience that why you need to take these things very seriously while on the road. For these reasons highlighting safety and checking things around the truck will keep you safe on the road this can help a lot of people stay safe. Well we rested up and when I woke up the next day knowing we still had to wait till Angel called. As i layed there i was thinking to myself that I sure did get some good sleep last night. Still knowing we still had to wait and i knew i still need to practice still being rusty with switching gears. I wanted to practice more on shifting so I decided to drive up and down the road while we were waiting there was a nice size hill on that road which came in handy for me. While I was going up and down the road to practice downshift and upshift so I could get the hang of it a little more. I thought this was pretty cool since we weren't doing anything anyway so i practiced for a little while then i parked the truck i didn't want to burn up that much fuel is what i was thinking After i stopped driving it was towards the end of the day because we did sleep in knowing we were over our 34 reset. Still waiting on the call from the boss so i gave him a call to see what was going on and he responded that we were still on standby and hell let me know as soon as he find out. So he hung up and we remained on standby. for the load confirmation by then we decided to grab us something to eat at that sta- tion were they sold that hot food togo of course. I had to get There baked chicken plate greens And cabbage of course gravy and fries to check how there's we're gonna taste because there food sure was bomb. I knew the food was gonna be good. As they made my plate i just ask them to make me a double plate so i can warm mines up letter and don't have to worry about eating on nothing tell we rolled out and so i didn't have to drive back down the way so we was good for the meantime while we were waiting. We got our food then headed back to the truck to eat up and of course i had to wait till we stopped and parked back at the truck stop to eat. As i got to eating my food i don't know if it's when the fries get soggy there bomber or when they're fresh out and crunchy with gravy are better. I don't know but i said they have some bomb food. It seemed like the food taste a little different from california food but it was good i tell you. Everyone seems to love it because when i looked up they had a line of people coming in for breakfast food. Breakfast sandwiches and they had made and other types of food. They had a good menu that had the whole town coming through seemed like. They had what they wanted and I tell you they made all kinds of stuff that looked good for breakfast to lunch and dinner. But i went with the thought I knew how hungry i was so i didn't wanna take any chances on anything nasty at that time. And I knew my father didn't wanna take that chance either plus we didn't have money to be wasting on anything. But we made it do what it do And i tell you that food had us nice and full it was just what we needed at that time. I'm thinking to myself at the same time saying i hope the boss calls and have a load for us in the morning. We headed down the road to park back at the truck stop so we would be well rested up for the next day. We got up early the next day and went into the the restaurant that was there at the truck stop. To get some breakfast we sat there for a while after eating and still waiting on that phone call from Angel so we headed back to the truck to wait on that call. As i layed down i started to think to myself this is just how truckers get fat if they out here eating like this all the time eat and don't do nothing else but drive and get ready to eat again. It didn't bother you much now but i also said to myself with all these food places that i never been to. I knew i was going all in to try and see how there food was and i would get back to that fat thought latter. As we laid there waiting on the call from the boss, while waiting on that call it seems like that makes all the difference in how your day will go and for a trucker that meant alot I started to see that for myself. But i knew adjusting wouldn't be that difficult since i wanted it that bad well at least that's what i thought. We pretty much rested that whole day that's when i got the call from the boss saying to head over to the ranch. To check in so they can start getting the load ready and he's about to send over the load confirmation so we can check in when we get there. So we headed over to the ranch to check in. It was towards the end of the day and after i checked in i asked was the load ready. Of course not nope they respond. I'm like ok so i knew it was going to be a another few hour wait just didn't know how long the wait was going to be the load wasn't ready they still were getting the load together so i knew that we were going to still be here till the early morning or so i pulled around to the parking waiting area and parked and set the reefer to the temperature the asked. You have to do this especially when picking up fresh meat. We Set it to 20 degrees to pre cool the trailer so we can get loaded. If the trailer wasn't to a certain temperature, they asked you to wait for the temperature to drop or they will not load the trailer, till the temp is set to the specific temp and the inside of the trailer is pre cooled. Before they load the load so we set the trailer to its temp then we jump back in to the truck to take a nape till they were ready to load us up. When i checked in i had to give them my phone number so there were gonna call me when they were ready for me to back into a door to get loaded. So i kept the phone close and up to my ear so i can hear the call when they called for us. We must of been waiting for about 7 hours before they called us to a door after we got to a door we still had to wait another four or five hours before they were done finishing loading us up then of course I had checked into the office to get the Paperwork for the load then went back to the truck to get the log book right so we could head down the road. This load we picked up had two drops one Iin San Diego CA and the second one in Corona CA. We headed out to trying and stay ahead of time. We weren't that far from that fuel stop that had the cheap fuel in meridian Mississippi with them having cheap fuel and having that restaurant was a plus specially that fish sand- wich and them fries And gravy so you know that we were stopping back buy grab a bite for sure and fuel back up. So I called the boss to get a com check for some fuel so he said he'll send right over in a few minutes we were low on fuel but we had enough to make it to the fuel stop we weren't too far from it but the time we got there he sent it over in a text message. So we fueled up and got our food from the restaurant we sat down and ate, before we headed out and of course I had to take me a order to go since I knew the the next food place that I knew of was still some hours down the road so I knew the sandwich would hold me over till then Not trying to go out of rought just to get something to eat, now don't get me wrong I would but my pops kept telling me that's not the best thing to do when you don't know your way around. With him telling me that I wasn't really trying to go out of rought then trying to get back on rought not knowing what street to turnonto to make it back in my direction. Can be a huge headache. I know I hate going the wrong way in a car when the gps guides you the wrong way but to be in a huge truck a And to go down the wrong street that is not a truck route can be a bigger headache I, know" so we just stayed on rought. By this time I've been getting better with shifting every time I got back into the truck things became smoother for me the more I did it the more it became more easier It's crazy how different things you think you can rush just won't work that way the only way it will work if you're taken your time this was a crazy way to highlight this situation, to me when trying to rush into something. To work but it was not working in that matter But strategy was a big thing to me always and know Ing my mission. That idea really stuck in my head when that happened to me. When that idea crossed my mind I always wondered why these thoughts would run threw my head with all I been through in my life for a min it started to hit me even after I heard it a thousand times before from different people. I'm really here to deliver a message I just didn't know what at the time. But what I did know that's it's in my heart to do what's right and by Any means and once I, opened "my eyes in a different way this may be confusing to some but another way I can say it is first I was blind but know what can see. Which was a real deep thought for me but I always kept these ideas highlighted with myself. But I enjoy every bit of what I was learning and the form I was learning it wasn't just no easy task because the rought I was taken wasn't no ordinary rought because if it was I think I would've run into more people with similar stories while I traveled the states on the road as a trucker, not saying there wasn't any, but rare to run into people with a similar story or to say the had the same situation happen to them this made me think it's all about who you know and what you know because the way I grew up I had to learn a lot buy getting the job done and doing what you needed to do if you wanted to make things happen or end met The more I traveled and the more people I ran into that I had conversations with highlighted to me the more I seen for myself I was very lucky n the position I was in. I kept in mind as I stayed focused on what I had to do to get to the next spot or I should I say level up. As we headed down the road we stopped about three hours at a flying J truck stop to stretch our legs and to use the restroom then continued down the road. When your clock starts you wanna use as much time up rollen down the road as much as possible to try and get the most miles out of the day. Which was every driver mission when behind the wheel. We kept the truck moving even tho it was two of us we still drove and took breaks. Just really trying to stay in good timing with the delivery. When we left Mississippi it didn't take us that long to get to Louisiana then back into Texas. We were still on i20 so as we got to Texas my sandwich just about to wore off and the BBQ joint was up ahead. We decided to go ahead and take our break there. We stopped and parked at the ♥ loves truck stop which was right behind the BBQ joint and parked and then went inside so we can sit down and enjoy our food there with not to many spots after passing this up we had to grab something from there. Just thinking of that good o food at the BBQ joint and the way they make there side dishes didn't do nothing but make me more hungry just thinking of the food. I mean they really get down on there food there it's a can't not pass if you're in this rough unless you don't have time to stop but once you do try it your gonna make time if your passing ex 540 on i20 J Bees BBQ joint (If you stop there after reading this let them know they were hightled in this book) So you bet soon as we got to the joint we we took out break. We went on in and ordered and sat down to enjoy our food the place is nice and relaxing music and air condition man i tell you this spot is it and of course i had to get me an order to go. Roast beef Sandwich With the bbq sauce on the side and a chicken plate to go and three sides. So we finished eating up and got ready to head back down the road didn't wanna leave that joint just yet but we had to go we had to keep things rolling cuz the clock is still tickin. We did like to keep things rollin to stay on time were we did not need to rush driving this big truck a lot of things can happen driven these trucks. When having to operate this thing you have to stay alert at all times be- cause you never know what may happen at any given time. My pops spoke on every safy tip he could and to keep me alert while he was with me just so i would know so i could be safe as i could be when i'm out on the road by myself. I really respected this time to where he was teaching me in a way to where i would understand. I been in a lot of training classes with different instructors. Even tho i was with my father and he was my in- structor. I'm glad that we were able to work things out because i see a lot of things happening in life with different families and friends. They couldn't get along to make things grow even with different family mem- bers in my family so i was really grateful that me and my father could work things out so i was able to go down the road by myself one day knowing how to handle myself out here on the road by myself. Which i wanted to do so bad so i just stayed focused on my mission to learn what i needed to learn to be successful if i was going to be doing this trucking stuff so i was really thankful how things was working out i keep saying this over and over again just surprised how things were flowing, How i just thought of something positive to do, and things start falling right into place I mean forreal right into place, on how i needed to handle my business that i really dreamed into reality' asking myself i wonder how the rest of my mission would turn out knowing i had a lot more to learn about the business knowing my pops knew how to operate the truck i still was going to need more training from someone who specializes in running a company and knowing the ins and outs. Staying focused and positive i knew i'm going to find the right people to help form a Huge successful business. I didn't know, but thinking about it that way made it kind of exciting to me when i thought about it that way. We drove for a good while that day and covered a nice amount of miles that day we stopped somewhere in Texas. At least that's how it feels when your driven threw Texas since it's so big we ended up stopping and another Loves on i20 to rest up and continue on our way back to California to drop. so that's where we'll take our ten our break to rest up and reset our work clock to continue for the next day. So we stop to rest up and I'm thinking of all this knowledge that my dad is given me while we're on the road I'm saying to myself it's a lot of stuff to learn out here and I knew it was way more information I had to learn from my father and so much information that he didn't know that I was still going to have to figure out how I was as going to make things work for me to get the information. I needed to run a successful trucking company even tho my father was helping me out a lot I still needed information to help build up a successful trucking com- pany. That's one of the reasons my father would keep telling me that I'm not ready to jump out and start my own trucking company with so much more to learn but that's not how I thought about getting started up I don't know what really ran threw my father's mind when he would think of me jumping out and started my own trucking company. But whatever it was as we were not thinking of getting started in the same form and I just knew I had to keep thinking of what I knew and use it best for me when the time was right. I would make the best decision to move forward when the time was right. Which being so determined to find the way that was going to fit for what I was trying to do. Seemed like I would fall asleep thinking about what I wanted to do. Things were very exciting for me, the change and a new way of living. Well we sat there and rested up and got up early the next day showered up and got ready to head, back down the road. In the meantime I had the call Angel to get another com check for fuel before we ran out just to keep things flowing in our rought. We waited for him to send it over still thinking to myself he doesn't really say anything but still sounds like he's having a rough day at least that's what I thought, still keeping in mind what my friend mentioned he was having household problems. Thinking to myself having problems while running a business can be a big distraction to your business and if you don't have responsible drivers things can really get bad out in this field that really highlighted to me I really thought about that as we made it down the road and fueled up and rolled on into California we made it to our first drop in good timing. We we're on time after checking in they got us straight into a door pretty fast and unloaded us in about 45 min then checked back in to the office to receive the Paperwork then headed off to the last drop which we made it there in good timing also which was great I wasn't trying to see how they deal with you when you're late so I'm glad we were making good timing. So when we arrived to the drop it was a small place to when we got there there was no other trucks there when we pulled up they were there waiting on us to pull up to get unloaded which I thought was great When I saw that I knew we was going to be there a short while plus they didn't have that many pallets to unload out of the trailer. As I sat there smiling I just couldn't wait to get back. To pick up that check easy money I consider it I was just so happy to get a fat check at least it was to me at least. From a vision that was made come true from making a change in my life as they took about 30 min to unload us. Then we headed back to the yard to park the truck. When we got to the yard Danny was there waiting for me to pull up, Danny was another driver who drove for Angel. He was there waiting to roll out in the truck to go pick up his load. As soon as I parked we start to unload all my stuff and pops was getting his stuff out of the truck that we had with us so we can keep up with our stuff. I don't think anybody wants to leave there stuff in the truck with other people when you're not headed out with them to go down the road with. I would always take my stuff out every time we got to the yard when switching up when getting out of the truck when getting back to the yard. At that time I didn't know howAngel ran his company but what I did find out that he did keept his truck moving. Which let me know you have to keep your truck moving, to make things add up after we got all our stuff out of the truck I check d In with Angel he heads out and walks around the truck still seeming upset to me but I didn't Even say nothing just went with the flow. After he did his walk around then he goes back in the office and ask when i'll be ready to roll out ? I responded when Danny got back, we'll he'll be gone for a week or so doing the same trip when he gets back you can roll back out that would be great so I agreed, while he got the check ready I talked to Danny for a minute then we both headed our way Angel came out and handed me my check so then we went ahead and rolled out. I headed to the bank the bank was right down the street I went on in to cash the check and came back out to give my pops his cut which only wanted me to give him only $500.00 my check my check was for 1500.00 which was for for the run out to ATL and back to California. I was really cool with how things played out I just got a job and don't know how to operate the truck and still got paid. I Was so happy with myself on how I made this happen and this was only the beginning of things. So after I gave my pops his money We hugged and he said he was headed to the house to go rest up and relax and to hit him up with in a day or so and we'll go out to eat or just put something out on the grill and talk about my ideas. Thinking to myself was a good idea and we get to spend more time together I did need more schooling for what was running thru my mind so I agreed and I responded I'll call you later and we'll talk that sounds great I'm about to go and get myself situated with myself and we'll talk so we headed out. I headed to the house my kids and girlfriend couldnt wait to see me and i couldn't wait to see and hug them and tell them more about my trip and my thoughts and how I pictured things in the future from a vision I had. My girl and kids were always interested in my ideas They always said I always have amazing ideas I would always share my ideas with them they love the way I tell stories they say I make crazy face impressions and make all kinds of side sound effects which I do but they sure let me know I can tell a story in a funny way. I would just be so, "excited to tell the story that I'm telling or I just love to express crazy moments, when this happen. But I knew I love to tell my stories I always wanted to let them in on what was going on in my mind. If I was right or wrong but the way I felt I liked to express that to them and let them know to always speak your mind but be respectful at the same time because right or righteousness will always overcome the wrong reasons if discussed on equal grounds. We always enjoyed our time together s we got ready to go out on our family day outing to enjoy our family time together. I always wanted to express my- self to my loved ones. That family time was really important and to treat your family right and with love and respect because it's a lot of people out here in the world that just treat people and family like it's no love and I didn't want that filling or vibes no were near me or what I had going on that's just bad energy that can lead to bad places is how I expressed that feeling and emotions when that came up when that idea came up. As We headed out they decided that they decided that we go eat at Loiselle BBQ. So that's where we headed to go and feed our face. When we got there we ordered our full course meal we sat there and ate up we got so stuffed our selfies no one felt like moving but we tightened up and headed back to the car to go and find the movie man because nobody wanted to do any- thing else after we ate which was cool with me. We ate good now we about to watch a few movies which was right up my alley some different movies to get us through these next nights couldn't get any better Family time is the best time it's what I like to express. Free time with the family we ended up finding the movie man we checked out what he had that was new that came out. We wanted to make sure that we got anof to keep up s bizzy for a few days and to catch up on the ones we haven't seen. when we pulled up on him he had a nice variety of movies to choose from he actually gave us 7 movies for $20.00 which I thought was cool plus 7 movies would have us bizzy for a nice amount of time. We grabbed some snacks and popcorn to head to the house, were about to have a nice time at the house catching up with a movie night for the next couple of nights because, we really picked out some good movies. That we had to catch up on because we loved to stay up on our movie game and storytelling, adventures and some rated R movies we had to go threw all of them. That's just what we liked to do together when it came to catching up when we didn't make into the theater. We loved to catch the theaters but sometimes we didn't make it. But hey, we loved it when it came down to movie night at the crib Which always turned into a small pizza party by the end of the night because of course. The kids talked the pizza up as the night fell so what could I say, Order up and make Sure you order my chocolate chip cookies. I had to have my cookie no matter, whatever went on so we made the best of it on what we had going on which I really liked about our time as I rested up on my time off at the house from being on the road. Driving all those miles to where you are tired even tho we had plenty of rest when we weren't driving. Since we could talk and understand what my change was like. I let them know that i was just gonna relax a little bit till i get back rollin because it really beat me up trying to get the hang of things so i just really ready just to relaxed and as I was in deep thoughts about what i had going on, and how. I was going to handle it. All i know is that this thought it stayed on my mind and i didn't know why but I kept thinking to myself i didn't know yet but i was going to figure it out and thinking i hope it's for the better for me. Meaning me becoming a better person just different thoughts running thru my mind. I always enjoyed my time off even tho i just got started and had a long way to go I still sat and thought to myself how can i do this all day and still make a great income. This stayed on my mind the whole time I was learning. As i rested up and the day was close to get ready to head back out because Angel called to let me know Danny. Will be back the next day in the evening and asked me if i would be ready to head back out? I replied, yes what time do i need to be at the yard he says after 6 or you can start in the morning and he has the load information already in hand so let him know I was like cool I'll call you back and let you know by noon tomorrow. He said cool talk to you tomorrow i'm like cool. Now I called my pops up to let him know to see if he was ready to roll out ? He was like what time I let him know what Angel said we could leave out tomorrow evening or the following day in the morning. Pops replied let's roll out tomorrow after the traffic so we don't get caught up in the morning traffic. I was like cool, I'm call Angel and let him know what time will be at the yard so we can get to the yard before everybody left the yard. So buy the time we got to the yard we got there was in good timing. Danny was still at the yard he was done taken his stuff out of the truck still at the yard talking to the fellas which was perfect timing so we parked and started to load up our stuff into the truck so we could head out. Me and Danny had a little conver- sation before we both headed out about how the truck ran and how things went for him out on the road. He replied another trip another dollar things went smooth rolled on down there and right on back truck ant have no problems. I'm like cool, Well it's time to roll out i get with you when we get back so me and pops got ready to roll out i had to talk with Angel before we headed out to get all the information on the load and he let me know he would give me the fuel advance after we got loaded up. Just give us a heads up Im like cool. So i got the information i needed and headed back to the truck to head out to pick up the load to beat the am traffic so we could start our day first thing in the morning at our first pick up. Which i like the fact that pops highlighted that starting the day in the morning at the pick up instead of the middle of the day, i liked it that way pops lined that up because starting your day at the shipper shure made since then starting in the middle of the day when you're trying to cover good miles and make it down the road and have enuf time to make it to the next shipper all in the same day. Just listening to my pops the way he said to do things really made since at the end of the day and by having someone that can walk you through certain situations to help you grow and one you feel comfortable with to train you and speak on a lot of things without. You Having to ask really meant a lot to me because I learned a lot of things by hands on training and i had to ask 101 questions just to learn and to figure out what was going on in a way that i was going to learn. I'm really aware of the way He's delivering this information to me As I took it into consideration when or if I came into being a trainer if that came to be. A lot of different things that i was deep thinking about always sat in my mind and i didn't know why but it was a feeling i had and never knew what this feeling was all i know is that the feeling wasn't no bad feeling but is was a feeling that i told myself that i was gonna find out on my own I knew i would one day find out with my self what this feeling was As we were on our way to the pick up my pops was driving and i was gonna start the next day so we made it to the pick up early. That morning so we could check in as soon as they opened. Things worked out how pops planned. To start the day right at the shipper really is a great way to start your day long as you have it planned out how you want things to flow unless something happen. He always said that things go wrong so when they do good always enjoy that time.

That day we made good timing getting to the picks we only had two picks which was cool with me, pops always said sometimes you might have three four or five picks depends on how the company wants you to run so yea the two picks was cool with me because the last load seemed like it took forever it took a lot of time picking them up it took a couple of days. Getting loaded pretty quick was cool with me Especially after the second pick up, we headed down the road At this time i'm driving now headed back down to head over the grape vine with me still learning how to downshift and still trying to keep an eye on the rpms while trying to shift. This was still a learning process for me especially with a heavy load loaded up in the trailer, but the process came to me the more and more i stayed behind that wheel but i was still in a learning stage. As we got closer to grape vine you can tell the truck starts to slow down by itself which lets you know it time to downshift when the rpms get to low as i paying attention to the rpms we were headed up the slop this grade reaches up to 4000 feet up to where your weight 44,500 will slow your truck all the way down to where you're climbing the incline at 25 or 35 mph or so with this amount of weight in your trailer as we got higher up the mountain this is where they say if you're a trucker then it's time to start trucking meaning you know how to operate your equipment to keep things moving and this is where trucking played its part as we slowed down i shifted to a lower gear at this point i'm still able to keep the truck moving up the incline as i'm climbing the hill slowly but surely. The biggest problem I had when it came to Trucking is to have the truck climb a steep incline which now I was mastering just like I do everything else I do so when he came to something that I put my mind to To take it in do deep thought and consideration which now I was mastering just like I do everything else I do so when it came to something that I put my mind toward to handle and was willing to make it work and was willing to make it work it didn't matter what anybody thought I knew I would make the best of it and have people amazed it didn't matter what anybody thought I knew I would make the best of it and have people that know me be amazed on how I do things. Again happy my father was there to help and assist me to where I was comfortable because if you're into Trucking and trying to learn having a good instruc- tor or one that can work with you and make you feel comfortable while you're learning is a big thing specially practicing and making mistakes and when your coach assist you but never they never gets upset or make you feel uncomfortable while you're in the driver seat even if you're spe- cially practicing and making mistakes to wear your coach asked you questions but never gets upset or make you feel uncomfortable while you're in the driver seat even if you're asking A handful of questions your- self that you may think might upset the instructor or just buy even con- stantly keeping grinding the gears as an instructor that can walk you through these steps without making it uncomfortable for you is a great coach. Learning this process was really a big impact when one can't train and work through all that and doesn't get mad with all that going on and remain calm and relaxed at the same time. really it made a big impact when someone was learning. When one can train and work through all that's going on with training and keeping the student alert and remain calm and relaxed at the same time really made a big impact when someone was learning that feeling I always kept in my mind saying to myself I would just add this to the knowledge as we slowly got to the top of the hill The more happier I got with myself thinking to myself, the higher I got the closer I thought I'm getting to where my dreams were coming true, is what was going through my mind I was so excited that I now know how to climb the steep hill in a truck. I was so happy for myself. Now I didn't know and now I know is the most joyful feeling you can have for yourself" especially when you know you had to make a change and had to put your mind to it and go to work to achieve what you told yourself from the start, is a feeling that can really let you tell yourself you can make anything happen when you put your mind to it and when you accomplish it. It is one of the most grateful feelings in the world when it comes to setting your goals and being persistent with things in life that you want to accomplish I'm telling myself I have to be riding some type of wave or something but." I'm writing this out" I'm telling my pops about this feeling, that I always I have when it comes to certain things that I'm doing and it never goes away unless I don't think about it My vision that I see and I'm trying my best to make come true. He says that's Allah talking to me letting me know that I'm on the right path of righteousness when you do the works that you're put here to do he'll let you know in a way that your on the right path but he talks to you in a way that you will know and no one else, so if this is the feeling that you have pay attention to the signs when the teacher talks he'll let you know In a way that your on the right path but he talks to you in a way that you will know and no one else so if this is the feeling that you have talking to you when the teacher talks you listen when you were giving instructions from the instructor you follow and pursue as a soldier that you are the message, the architect the master builder when you were given instructions from the instructor you follow and pursue as a soldier that you are the message the architect the master builder is The works I prayed for while you were in your mother's stomach I told you that I prayed and prayed so follow the steps from our leader all praises due to Allah. so you have to play your part in order to receive your blessings in order to remain the Messenger in the works for the people of righteousness you have to play your part in order to receive your blessings in order to remain the Messenger in the works for the people of righteousness. Everyone has their duty here on earth and when you find your duty and it is highlighted for you in life, now the question stands will you fall in suit and be the messenger our will you fall for the works of the devil which is the opposite of righteousness everyone has their duty here on earth and when you do anything other than righteous- ness that is and is the devil's work in a battle for what is right I always listen to my pops for what he said and what he talked about because me myself I was for the righteousness of things I tried doing what was right for the people when it came to where I could help one another for some- thing or do Something for them I was always with doing what's right for the people when it came to where I could help one another out with something so doing the wrong when it came to helping someone I was really against it when something had to do with all the good feelings I've been having just made me feel good on the inside and just to give myself more energy to keep my vision alive so I just keep doing what I've been doing and that's just keeping things flowing which we know slow motion is better than no motion I kept in control of the truck on the way coming down the grapevine with theses good feelings I've been having just made me feel good on the inside and it just gives me more energy to keep my vision alive so I just kept doing what I've been doing and that's just keep- ing things flowing, which we know slow motion is better than no motion I kept in control of the truck on the way coming down the grapevine The steep incline will have you burn out your breaks if not staying in full control of your truck so I kept us at a slow enough pace so I would not burn up the brakes staying in full control of your truck will keep you at a safe speed zone when loaded heavily you can't reach dangerous speeds so staying in control was a big safety condition while climbing in coming Down a steep incline. A incline will have you burn out your brakes if not staying in full control of your truck so I made shure I kept us at a slow enough pace so I would not burn out or heat up the brakes to much while staying in full control of your truck will keep you in safety zone when Loaded heavily you can reach danger speeds speeding or rushing down a hill with a heavy load so staying in control was a big safety condition while climbing in coming down A steep grade. If you never operated a truck if you you never Felt the weight of something push you while you're driving one of these bad boys. It sure will let you know how that feels which can be scary. You only know this feeling if you drove one. As we made it to the bottom and I drove us all the way to Arizona. since we down the road last few trips and I noticed where the stops were we stopped at before we pretty much made the same stops on the way out to the delivery to Atl Atlanta the trip went pretty smooth on the way we didn't have any truck problems or anything. We ended up making the same few stops to get fuel so when I got ready to call in to "get the fuel Advance this particular time when I called in Angel finally had something to say. Not after really having any conversations with him he says he will send it over in a minute he says but I don't know what is going on but I'm spending too much money on fuel when he says this I responded how was that he says I don't know how but I'm spending more on fuel then before then he said I have to go, I'll send it over in a minute then hangs up the phone. After he hangs up I say to my Pops he says that I'm burning too much fuel. Pops" Says how does he come up with that I say I don't know. Pops says see that's why you need to suck all this information up because you're lucky to get all this information for the way I'm getting into the trucking industry because you don't get into no driving job the way I did. This is real I've been out here a long time and you don't always look up this easy the way I did to get a job and to go straight to work without anyone checking my work performance so

I was really lucky to proceed the way I did so I needed to suck all this information up because you never know how quick things can change so don't let that man get you upset or off track you got a plan you have to be ready for the sudden changes In this when you're not in full control so just listen to the man don't let him get you fired up and just ride this out the devil is trying to get you out of character so don't let that grab your attention. Well get down there and deliver the load and see what he has to say when we get back now when you call him back when you need to call him don't let him get yourself out of character I know how you can get. I know Pops but I can handle it, you know he was pissing me off when he was on the phone Pops but he can only say what he wants but I have a plan for that pops pops is like no, you have to suck all this up so you know how to function when you're out here by yourself I'm like I know Pops but this guy doesn't know my hustle. Pops is like you can't think like that I'm like Pops what you mean this guy doesn't know me like that I'm have my own truck in a minute Pops is like you need to learn a whole lot before you get your own truck I'm like I'm learning now how much learning do you think I need I'm not the average person doesn't take me long to catch on pops is like just listen you need to learn a lot before getting your own truck I'm like OK Pops. I'm listen- ing but I know my Pops doesn't know me that well so I let him talk and do his father thing but at the same time I was thinking in the back of my mind that I would figure this thing out how I will start my own company and get things going trying to explain that didn't meet no one's view, from me saying that everyone thought I was moving too fast. But for now I have a way where I will be able to make some cash and gain a lot of knowledge for, just getting in this industry, so I could make a step up in this industry if he cut me off it wouldn't be a problem but I couldn't get that out of him so I listen and let him show me his ways of doing things but I will be putting my twist on things when the ball falls back into my hand to make a decision by me knowing my dad didn't know my hustle I just let him continue to show me different ways to proceed I was a good listener so I did just that. We filled up at exit 100 and kept rolling into Tucson Arizona to the" Triple T truck" stop to do our reset before we kept driving to rest for the day we stop there so we can get a good meal from the restaurant in which. We ended up ordering steak and eggs for dinner which was cool with me they seem to make it real tender and juicy so that was all good with me. We enjoyed our dinner We Showered up and then went back to the truck so we can get rested up so we can start another early day starting early in the morning was kind of cool so by the end of the day you wouldn't have to drive around the truck parking lot in circles for 20 or 30 min just to find a parking spot so the early morning start was great when you could keep that going specially the way that things worked out on the highway depending on which part of the city you're in when starting your day. We rested up and got up and did our safety check on the truck and trailer then started our day we rolled right through New Mexico right on into Texas we took Highway I 10 to high- way I 20 on through Texas we had to stop at a few stop in Texas to get fuel and some snakes then maded it to Meridian Mississippi so of course I had to call Angel he would only send enough of at this time just to make it to the next fuel truck stop. Which kept me thinking : which I thought was strange but I guess that's how he did things but still was accusing me of stealing fuel. the truck should not be burning that fuel I responded and let him know I don't know why but I'm putting all the fuel advance that you're sending me into the truck I don't use none of I been putting the fuel where it supposed to go so I don't see how you're saying that, "that I must be stealing the fuel or selling it and what he started to say this time which I thought was really strange to me but he sent it over and was pretty upset as always and really trying to get me to argue with him. I was not falling for it my pops was surprised that I was not getting upset with Angel but as soon as I hung up boy was my mouth going off, he he was really pissing me off assuming that And telling me what I was doing the whole time I was being honest with him I was so mad I had to call my friend that got me the job, just to let him know what I was going through to see if this is how he works or what was going on because I was getting un- comfortable driving this man's truck and he's has all this to say I don't know if the truck is just burning more for you than usual or what but he keeps saying that I'm stealing the fuel or selling it and that is really pissing me off he replies man I'll give him a call and see what he's talking, about and he call me back and let me know what the deal is, I'm like let me know something because this dude is really on one. He's ike he'll hit me back I'm like cool talk to you in a minute so we hang up and I continue down the road to make good miles for the day we knocked out our hours for the day and ended up on the other side of Texas at the end of our work shift so we did a reset at a Love's Truck Stop before we continue our trip and of course we had to stop at the barbecue joint to get some grub but we still had a few hours to drive to get there so we scheduled to be there tomorrow by the time we get there they'll be open will be pulling up getting ready for them as they should be getting ready for us I tell you I will not pass this place up if I'm coming through this way on I 20 through Texas it's a must stop if you're going to pass exit 540. We rested up and made our way down the highway we made it to the barbecue place about 10:30 AM they were wide open waiting for us to pull up just what I like a place waiting for you when you pull up to get busy. Starting off making my plate we were kind of early So they weren't that busy but they did have people in there this early getting there grub on that's how they're getting it II was surprise the line wasn't that long, with the quick service they had was really great specially when trying to keep up with the clock and not waste tha much time so the service there is a really great, right along with the food they're serving you so we tightened up on our food and yeah we ordered a order to go a roast beef sandwich with the sauce on the side so my Bread doesn't get soggy when it's time for me to eat it. Also a barbecue chicken plate to go. Then headed back to the truck to get ready to head back down the road with a big smile on my face and nice and full. Then Pops says you are not playing about that joint you're going to make sure you stop there every time I see. I'm like Pops you bet I haven't found a place like it in our rough so tell then, this will be the spot Till i find an- other one if you have another one in mind let me know so we can try it out please, the way the food taste when you leave Calli is different taste from Cali that makes it a little more interesting to taste what they have to offer Pops says he didn't really know any more spots to eat like that the best thing to do is keep an eye open for another one or look one up that might be in route that were moving in and I'm like oh if I'm trying to look for one I will have to look one up to see if one was in my route but no biggie I'm ready for whatever we pass up or ready to taste it if it's something I'm thinking about trying I like to try different things out on the road but really picky about a lot of foods also so I try and make things work if I could you know how people can be about their food and ♥ I'm a real picky person if I might say but not too difficult to deal with, as I laughed out loud as we got back rolling I knew we weren't too far from our. Drop about another day or so driving but we were making good timing we stayed rolling but again it was time to call Angel to get a fuel advance from him already saying what he was saying. I didn't even want to call him back to let him know. That we needed more fuel just off his attitude but I had no choice to keep things moving to stay on time. To get to the drop so I gave him a call to let him know, It was just what I thought he had something to say now I'm really thinking to myself some- thing was up when I get back to the yard I'm not sure if I am even going to roll back out in this man's truck, is what I was telling my father now Pops is like just roll with the punches you're already blessed you got a job got rolling now you know how to operate the truck so just relax I'm like I'm good telling my father, now" Pops says again just roll with the punches you're already blessed you got a job got rolling now you know how to operate the truck so just relax I'm like I'm good pops but I just not with all the accusing I'm not stealing or doing anything I'm not supposed to be doing I'm telling you Pops I can make something happen in a good Way for me I just need a little more training he replies you need a lot, I'm like I know that but I just need a little more to get what I need to get started Pops is like what are you talking about Im like Pops somethings is kind of hard for me to explain right now but I will be able to explain it to you later. Just my hustle is hard to explain when no one really sees the vision but you so it's like one of these things that I have to show you in- stead of telling you somethings are better much done then said if you know what I mean you know. The way you view things in your mind when no one else can understand you or try to see things your way when you have nothing to show or prove at the time but don't worry. Pops I will sure let you know what time it is. Just then Angel text over the fuel ad- vance so we could fuel up and continue to make it down the road which was cool because we stayed in motion and didn't have to sit and wait for a long time for him to send itI Was I just rolling with the flow but this time we only have about six or seven hours before we made it to Atlanta GA to our drop which wasn't bad the only bad thing was this dude has an attitude and now got me thinking if he's trying to play with my money when I get back when is time to pay me. Pops is like no no you don't think that way don't think like that. "Pops "know how I can get so he's always trying to let me know how to handle a lot of situations I'm like Pops I'm just thinking out loud I don't let this guy know how I'm really feeling that's why I hang up before I let you know how I feel about what he's saying based on how things are going now but I'm riding this out plus we're almost to the drop that means we're halfway through the week as we speak so I'm telling you Pops I'll be straight I just know I had to learn how to operate things and everybody can say that 'm not ready to jump outside the box. But I know what I can make happen out of nothing pops says, OK if you say so I'm like pops you'll see how I make things happen when I put my mind to it. When I really put my mind to something" that's my motive I give to myself" and how I work when I put my mind to something I really follow through I already have everybody amazed Buy the things I do, Now and how I know it's real. I always tested myself when I was young with many obstacles I always challenged myself when I was younger and always succeeded when I did so whatever I was doing. I felt like this was just another obstacle on a different level. "I felt like I was really ready to attack this I always seem to amaze so many people with thinking I can do something in any field once I put my mind to it as we made it to that fuel stop. We fueled up and continue down the road made our way into Atlanta Georgia for our drop and we made it there a little early before they opened to check and see if we were at the right location sometimes you have to make sure your at the right building some can be close to each other or sometimes in the same building with differ- ent check in windows when we pulled up to the address we just hung out in the parking lot since they were still closed so we had to wait a little bit before they opened up in the morning to check in to get unloaded. The wait wasn't so bad. As it got closer to the end of a day and it was time to reset anyways now. Things went pretty smooth. We were cool. It was all good with me and Pops and how time is going. It was nothing really around when we got there. Put a line of truck of course after they opened up and I went in and checked in to get unloaded. The wait wasn't that bad. It took them about two hours and a half to unload us then I called Angel i to let him know the load was delivered clean. So he lets us know to go ahead and rest up and he'll call when he receives the load confirma- tion, I ask we're we'll be going to be picking up at, he'll Call back as soon as he receives it. Then let us know where we will be headed out to. I was like ok cool talk to u later after we headed out to the closest truck stop to rest up shower up and relax till he gave us a call to let us know where we're gonna be picking up from. He called back in a few hours and let us know to head out to Mississippi that's where we'll be picking our load up at from the chicken ranch, so go ahead and head back to the same truck stop and rest up tell they're ready to call you to a door but the load doesn't pick up tell Monday, it was Saturday morning so we had plenty of time to make it to Mississippi before we had to check in so we had plenty of time to break before we headed over there. We Headed to the closest truck stop to rest up before we headed to Mississippi we ended up take a break at a loves trucks stop on i20 before headed out. To shower up grab a snake then we headed out threw Alabama and right on into Mississippi to wait at the truck stop that we were at before so will be closer To the pick up address for Monday so we could check in early and get down the road Angel call back to let us know he was getting ready to send the info over and if we was ready to roll out. ♥♥♥♥♥♥ I replied yup so he was like cool I'm about to send over the info so y'all can head over to check in. He sent the pick up info right over then we headed out to go ahead and check in to the chicken ranch, they let us know that it we'll be a some hours before we got a door so we pulled a around to the other side of the ranch were we could park and wait for them to call us : to back into a door so we pulled around and found a spot to park. Then waited till they gave us a call to go back into a door we had to wait for about Seven hours before they called us when they did, we pulled around to the door they asked us back into to get loaded. Once we opened the doors to the trailer and backed in. I got back into the truck to finish getting some rest before it was time to roll out since we've been sitting for a while, It will be time to hit the road by the time we're done. Keeping up with the time, we'll be ready to be back on duty. When it comes to logging back on and keep- ing a record of the driving log book. As we waited I knew it would be a few more hours before they were going to be done loading us up and it was still early in the morning. I went ahead and went back to sleep to rest up a little more before they called us up to tell us they were done loading us up.

As I went back to sleep and man was I getting some good sleep it seems like soon as your get into the deep sleep yup that's just when the phone rings with dispatch on the line saying that your all done getting loaded pull around to the office and pick up your paperwork and you'll be ready to roll out so we got up and pulled the truck forward so we could shoot the doors on the trailer to keep the temperature were it needs to be then pulled around to the office to get our load paperwork and to get our seal for the trailer then we headed out to head on our way back to California and I tell you it's something about that feeling that you get when you know you're headed back home that makes you feel good about what your accomplish while you are gone. As we headed back down the road to make it to the main highway since we were out in some little country town, well that's what it seemed like to me being from the city in all driving through these little towns in different parts of the south. A lot of towns looked so country that you really had to pay attention while driving because just seeing how people live and work still in a lot of older buildings in different states can be a real sight see since it's a different look from the city which will have you really looking around while driving thru these parts, not saying that I'm not aware of things when I'm driving but it's just something about sight seeing when passing thru these types of towns. Since we got an early start our day which was good I knew we should make it to Texas before our shift was over. As we headed through town and towards the highway we cruised on threw just absorbing up as much sightseeing as we headed down the highway westward towards California. We weren't that far from the state line To louisiana which only made us a few hours from Texas. I always used Texas as a halfway mile marker when traveling from the west coast to the east coast and back, So knowing that we were almost to our halfway mark was a good feeling. Also knowing we weren't that far from you know what ...Yes Our BBQ spot which was Great since we been rolling it was about time to eat and I was definitely starving as we cruised on in and rolled right in to loves parking lot to park and take or break we walked right in to the BBQ joint to grub on down we got in line yo order and of course I had one for here and one to go I'll pick my second order up after I'm done eating here. so I didn't have to get back in line which was cool with them so we both order and sat on down to enjoy our food and watch a little tv while we ate we ate up and got something to drink to go with my order then We headed back to the truck to put our food up. Then went into the the truck stop to grab a few more snake then we headed back to the truck to head on back down the road. We had a hole lot of miles to go so yea we wanted to keep track of the time which the way we stayed a head of things kept us pretty much good with keeping up with the time As we drove on down the highway staying on schedule driving through Texas since it is the biggest state we tried to stay rolling damn I 20 oh and into Dallas we stopped at the TA took a break stretched her legs use the restroom got a little fuel and back on down the highway we went we had a few more hours to drive through the state of Texas speed limit is a little higher than other states so we stay rolling Road right on and to El Paso we stopped at the Petro Truck Stop El Paso to stretch our legs again got us a few more things and they were long is the restaurant we headed on back to the truck I don't back down the road head on into New Mexico Mexico is not that big so we only spent a couple hours driving through New Mexico and then right on into Arizona we will be driving to Arizona for about four hours as we cruised all through we may one last few stop in Arizona took another short break that we had it all back into California once we got to California we was a few hours to the drop which bus breaking in fueling and continue down the highway we are doing pretty much great on the time looks like will be pretty much on time fr our drop which is pretty cool just knowing you're on time feels a whole lot better than the one you're late so Stan ahead of the clock and keeping your eye on the clock is a good thing out here on the road as we got to our drop on time I got out went in and checked in for our appointment once they found us on the chart told us to back into the door so they're gonna notice which is great we didn't really have to wait too much time to get unloaded got right in about a couple hours or so to get unloaded and headed home back to the yard I'll see what the boss was talking about I was really much excited that I really came this far from just I thought of wanting to change now I will park the truck at the yard and head into the office to see what the boss has to say out of all we've been through and driving down the road I want to see what he has to say Took us about 15 minutes to park the truck last 20 minutes so we can get our stuff out the truck as we tightened up getting the rest of our things out the truck and putting in a vehicle checked in to the office Angie was in the office on this phone as we entered the office so we walked in knowledge each other sat out I'll wait for him to get off the phone it's signed up this conversation as I notice he wasn't so excited to see me or something just seems strange usually he had my check ride over a point to let me know it's in the box with this day it didn't go the way it normally way he seem to have numerous of things he wasn't happy about traveling up and down the road with me being the driver he was saying things wouldn't happen the way they normally Adam so you let me know then he was gonna give me a call when he was ready for me to come back and get in the truck that didn' Sam like he wanted to call me back those are the dogs that ran through my something just didn't feel right about the way he said that so I agree grab my check sugar sand don't think you and I'll see him later and I love thinking to myself why would he say he will call me back when he was ready for me to get back in the truck instead of coming back next week I started to think and I really thought that was the end of my first training session but it really didn't bother me too much because I did have bigger plans A week or so passed I haven't got any phone calls to come back to the truck so I knew at this time I had to make another decision Which was that I was going to go fully independent everyone I spoken to about this decision told me not to do it but something just told me this is something I need to do so once I made that decision that I was fixing to go fully independent that's when I decided to go out and explore and see if I can find a truck that would work for me So I went back home I lived in Compton California when I was younger me my mother my 3 kids and a few kids from the Nabor hood started a program called COMPTON Junior Posse which now now they're called the COMPYON cowboys This program that we started and with my mother fully running the program started getting older in the years with me having kids at such a young age with me have to change my financial situation a little bit more than others I focused on my way to help me out to find a way to become more financially stable as my mother got older and years in the program steel to be going on my mother handing at the program down to my little cousin. Now my little cousin runs the program with everything being handed down to him with the ways he likes to operate it's a little different than when we

Ranett we focus on the question writing now they just doWest- ern riding and simple trail rig Western riding and simple trail rides which we are still located in the city of COMPTON continuing to support the youth and upcoming cowboys and cowgirls. Attending different camping trips different trail rides Playdays rodeo's and just hanging out with A lot of the neighbors and family and friends in the neighborhood we grew up with,. We Had a nice number amount of horses at the house as I was off the road and haven't been called back in to go back over the road I Continue To clean horse stalls at the ranch we have a ranch back at the house where we had about 15 to 20 horses so every morning I would get up go out to the ranch clean horse stalls make sure they were fed and watered this is my job till I figure out how to get back on the roadWhich I was fixing to find a way to get back down the road going fully independent this was something I had set my mind to and that I was going to accomplish to make these changes in life that I've been looking for be financial stable and to support my family after I got up every day clean stalls II will go out and drive around to different truck lots and a few different auctions that I would go to when I will try to flip a few cars trying to make some extra cash so I road around to these few places and just so happens I get to the last car action to stop and see if they possible to even have a truck in there for sale just so happens Igo in to speak to the owner which I knew for quite some time and he says to me you're looking for a big rig what made you want to look for Big Rig I gave my little story about I want to make a change in life and Trucking with something that interest me to where I could make a continuous amount of income and not struggle so much so he says oh yeah I say yes he says well I have a truck back there sitting on my lot a repo last month the guy was supposed to come pick it up yesterday yesterday was his last day to pick it up until I put a lien on it so I started to lean process he hasn't came back down to talk to me about it you can go out back and check it out tell me what you think if you like it let me know and probably can work some out the guy has all his stuff in there but check it out if you think you can work with it it's all back let me tell you now the truck does need some work to it but you can get it going that's what you wanna do go out back to the 2nd yard check it out come back and let me know what you wanna do so I went out back to go check the truck out which is a surprise to me soon as I say I wanted to do something seem like all pieces started to fall together I've never no one time the owl be checking out a diesel truck and a car auction that I buy cars it just so happens this one here when I am looking for one wow so as a stroll on route to the 2nd yard to go check the truck out to the yard it's a truck sitting over here big red faded color so when I walked up to the truck over the door I looked on the inside there's a lot of words they're fucked her truck wasn't really miss new parts but he said The truck did have some problems so I checked it out went back into the office and let him know hey I'm interested in the truck I said i'm a call my mechanic and see when he can get down here so he can check it out so he can let me know what kind of problems I'm looking at and if the guy doesn't come back and buy his truck I'm gonna buy this truck so I'll call you tomorrow and let you know what my mechanic says when can you come down and check the truck up and I appreciate you give me an a chance to grab his truck off your hands if the owner doesn't come and get it implies you got that give me a call tomorrow let me know what you wanna do so you can get that bad boy up of my lot you bet call you tomorrow I'll have to tell you're on my way back to the house :-) surprise just feeling some type of feeling I never felt before just know the feeling was telling me I was headed in the right direction so I have it all happy smiling got to the house just so surprised and feeling good about this new direction I'm headed in seeing like everything was just Flowing together I got home and gave My Mechanic i called his phone first time it went to voicemail the first time I called Soon as I hung up my phone started ringing that was him calling me back hey Mr Bill how's it going hey how's it going Who's this this is KD hey what's up KD how's it going oh man calling you man you know I'm always working on something oh man what you working on well I'm trying get my own big rig i I need you to come take a look at this big rig and let me know what would it take to get this thing down the roadHe says well I'm busy tomorrow I'll come by there Thursday Thursday morning about 10 I'm like cool that's fine he says where is the Truck I say it's only about 10 minutes from the house text me the address I'll meet you over there about 1030 OK great cool I'll text you the address see you to- morrow at 10:30 we both hang up again and I'm sitting here smiling surprised happy just thinking to myself how things are really flowingSo the next day in the morning a call back up to the yard to let the owner know that the mechanic can come by tomorrow at 10:30 in the morning and meet me up there he's like oh fine see you guys tomorrow at 10:30 then I asked if the guy called you about his truck he replies no the guy still hasn't called me about his truck I'm like OK cool see you tomorrow 10 30 so as I continue to do my regular routine I got up a little extra early the next day to get my stores taken care of so I would be done by 10:30 to meet Mr Bill at the light is that time things up the next morning by 10 o'clock get ready to meet Mr Bill up at the light got up to the light 1030 on the dot Mr Bill was pulling up great Mr Bill I am Mr Bill how's it Goin Aaa is it goingWe gotta go around back to go check the truck out so we had around back for around the pool is gages out that we're going around to the back and try to crank the truck up we noticed that the truck needs some batteries I wanna have some batteries poor from Off Ron side of one of the buildings from the storage unit getting charged up a little bit got him into the truck got the truck the turnover truck cranks over we are listening to the truck truck stone out a little bit of white smoke truck runs for a minute and put it on the computer small diagnose those a couple of coa we got to go around back to go check the truck out so we had around back put around the police gauges out that was going around to the back and try to crank the truck up we noticed that the truck needed some batteries only has batteries pulled from offer on side of one of the buildings from the storage unit got charged up a little bit got them into the truck got the truck the turnover truck cranks over we are listening to the truck truck stone out a little bit away smoke truck runs for a minute put it on the computer small diagnose those a couple of cods runs for a minuted then he says I can turn it off Mr Bill replies oh yeah trucks gonna need a lot of work $3000 for sure OK so I don't think it to myself mechanic said if you get this truck do you know it will be a project I replied thanks Mr Bill and he gives up his tools we head out to the yard back to the office go back in I asked the owner I'm interested in the truck how much you wanna sell the truck for he replies give me three grand and take the truck I say to myself you got a deal but I need you to give me two weeks to come back and get the truck he replies no problem I hold the truck for you because I don't think that guys coming back to get his truck if he was he would have come and got it already but I hold it back there in a bag for you you got two weeks I reply OK I'll be back in two weeks again I head back to the house my love cheese just thinking to myself things are flowing in two weeks I've been and picked up my second paycheck clean the stores and I might have to borrow a few dollars but I will be back in two weeks to get the truck so for the next two weeks I got up clean stalls fed horses make sure they were watered same program and count my dollars making sure I was gonna have enough in two weeks to get this truck so I know how much I was going to be getting on my paycheck and I was a few hundred dollar short so I have to get all my extra hassle and see who and where I can get some extra cash from Cel after I clean stalls I fed the horses I went out and found some small work for me to do to make some extra cash just so happens An old client call me up and ask me if I can replace the floor in there bathroom and if I can come by and give them an estimate which was like just right in time they were getting their floor replaced for a great price and I was going to make enough money to have the extra cash to pick that truck up so I ended up working on a small project which was only gona take me a few days to do which means I'll make that few extra cash and two weeks was back at the yard with the cash for the truck when I thought about it the way I fixed a car up every year me always fixing up a car, Lowrider meaning spending money on a car buying TVs paint job beat it was noth- ing for me to make this truck my next project What was so crazy is the same truck that I was driving up and down the road for the company is the same exact truck that I'm buying from the lot A 10 speed freightliner century After two weeks passed I went back to the lot to pick the truck up as I was talking to the owner he says the guy never called back to ask or even tried to get his truck back so it's good as yours so I paid him what he asked for the truck he put a few batteries in the truck Let them charged up enough to start. the truck was able to driveSo I started the truck up let it run for a bit got it in gear and head on back to the house a little bit on the white smoke came out the pipe but we made it home back to the yard at the house to park the truck then start making me a check out list on things that I was going to need to get the truck up and running and safe to be able to go back down the road once I got back to the house I was just so surprised and happy with myself on how I came up with a solution and things just really been falling together and now I'm putting the rest of the pieces together I feel so good to attack and handle something that you really want to do the biggest shock to me to myself which shocked others and that don't let nobody tell you you can do what you want to do every- body told me that I can't get a truck I'm not ready for truck but I told myself We are not the same I mean I felt like I was knees deep I got the truck now next mission is to check this boy out and get things together and get going since this is something new to me to attack And going through the motor getting the right parts for the motor and getting the motor up and running and being able to listen to how the motor sounds learning more of how the engine runs just really going through it mechan- ically I will be able to save money in the future just knowing more about the motor in my truck and how it runs and operates so yes the lessons begin me learning the inside and out of my truck all parts nuts bolts belts alter- nator starter water pump piston rings it was a whole list of things not just only to know the part but how to put the parts on and take them off I need to while going through this truck. was going to be a real valuable lesson for me not only just to be able to operate the truck but being able to attack different problems that would occur with the truck while I was driving it over the road I would have more of a understanding of how to fix things myself since I'm real good with my hands being handy and fixing things I was learning more than just how to operate Learning everything how to up and run a trucking company and how to handle all types of problems when they did happen when I did talk to other drivers about their trucks when they did have problems they would always say that they are calling they possibly get a tow truck towed out and they get towed into the shop if they can't make it to the shop pretty much that was it they didn't really know too much of how to attack anything that went wrong with the truck while on the road so with me learning a lot more than the average driver when I did talk to them about the things I had to doBeing the owner taken in on all responsibilities, was really a shock to them," for me taking full responsibility of being fully independent owner operatorSpecially when they doubt it me for even having the thought of going fully independent As my new journey begin with learning the full responsibility of being Fully independent in such a short period of time in which the took other drivers i talked to took the proses up to 5 to 6 years or even more some- times before they pick to go fully independent so the next few years of my life behind the wheel will be very exciting and an experience lesson to learn from to be continued

SINCE THE LATE 2005 I Khafra Akbar, has been respected for helping individuals to jumpstart their careers into the trucking industry the fully independent owner operator. Helping walk them through the unique challenges and opportunities that men and women face when trying to get started when going fully independent. Not leased to a company but in full control and running their own independent com- pany. After I spent my first few years getting into the trucking industry as a new Career in the highly competitive world of commercial trucking learning different steps and different ways to stay up and running when things and times can be difficult to stay up and running these different strategies that cost me so much time and money. I Khafra Akbar has used My service throughout the United States to help men and women to help them think more deeply about their lives out on the road and the time there spending working for the income there already making For the company there driving for. To see a big difference from working for a huge company to going fully independent you'll See a huge difference when you look at the invoices when getting paid. In 2004 I Formed TruckDriverCoach as a go to page for help on the internet which for the last five years or so I've helped dozens of individuals to jump Start their Carriers into the trucking industry to different levels into the trucking industry. During this time they became drivers for different companies some started their own companies from startup to purchasing their own truck and trailers and or just purchasing their own truck to be leased on to a company or just got there company up and running because they were just the investor and having a driver drive for them. At this time, I had connected with different companies. As different people came to me for my coaching services also helping some who came to me to help grow their companies. Working together when drivers came to me for help in finding a job I would direct them to the companies I've been in contact with. Threw my speaking and writing adds I've advertised. I have become a tireless advocate for women and men encouraging and inspiring them to jump Start their Career into the trucking industry. Even the people that been in the trucking industry for decades

TruckDriverCoach.com

TRUCK DRIVER COACH PROVIDES INDUSTRY expertise with passion, purpose, and persistence in the educational and professional development in the trucking, providing world class services and staffing and advocacy for the trucking industry. Our vision is to become the worldwide premiere organization offering seven-star pro- fessional training for our members.

StunazPeak
Business Coach

Hello,

My name is Khafra Akbar, I am the C.E.O of STUNAZPEAK. I have developed a strong reputation that's highly driven, dependable and com- mitted. My team and me are pursuing serious individuals become more successful. We'll conquer at competitive business levels that will help you be more successful.

Thank you for your time and consideration,
Khafra Akbar
C.E.O
Email: Khafratdc@gmail.com

www.ingramcontent.com/pod-product-compliance
Lightning Source LLC
Chambersburg PA
CBHW051230120626
46547CB00013B/1587